Choral Conducting
The Forging of the Conductor

Alberto Grau

GGM Editores was founded in 2002 with the goal of editing and distributing the work of composer and choral conductor Alberto Grau through the publication of his compositions and arrangements, numbering approximately 150 works. These include original compositions, arrangements, and orchestrations, among which the best-known works have been published by GGM.

Exclusive Rights
1st Edition, june 2005 - Spanish
2nd Edition, july 2009 - English
© GGM Editores, S.C.
ISBN: 0-9621532-9-X

GGM Editors / Earthsongs
e-mail: mariaguinand@hotmail.com • flormar@cantv.net
Web: http://www.fundacionscholacantorum.com/

Editorial Production: GGM Editors / Earthsongs
Graphic Design: Alicia Martínez Pais • aliciamartinezpais@gmail.com
Musical Examples: Flor Angélica Martínez Pais • flormar@cantv.net
Cover: S/T - (1970) Original engraving by Luisa Palacios
Cascade Printing
2.000 copies

To my life companion and colleague,
María Guinand

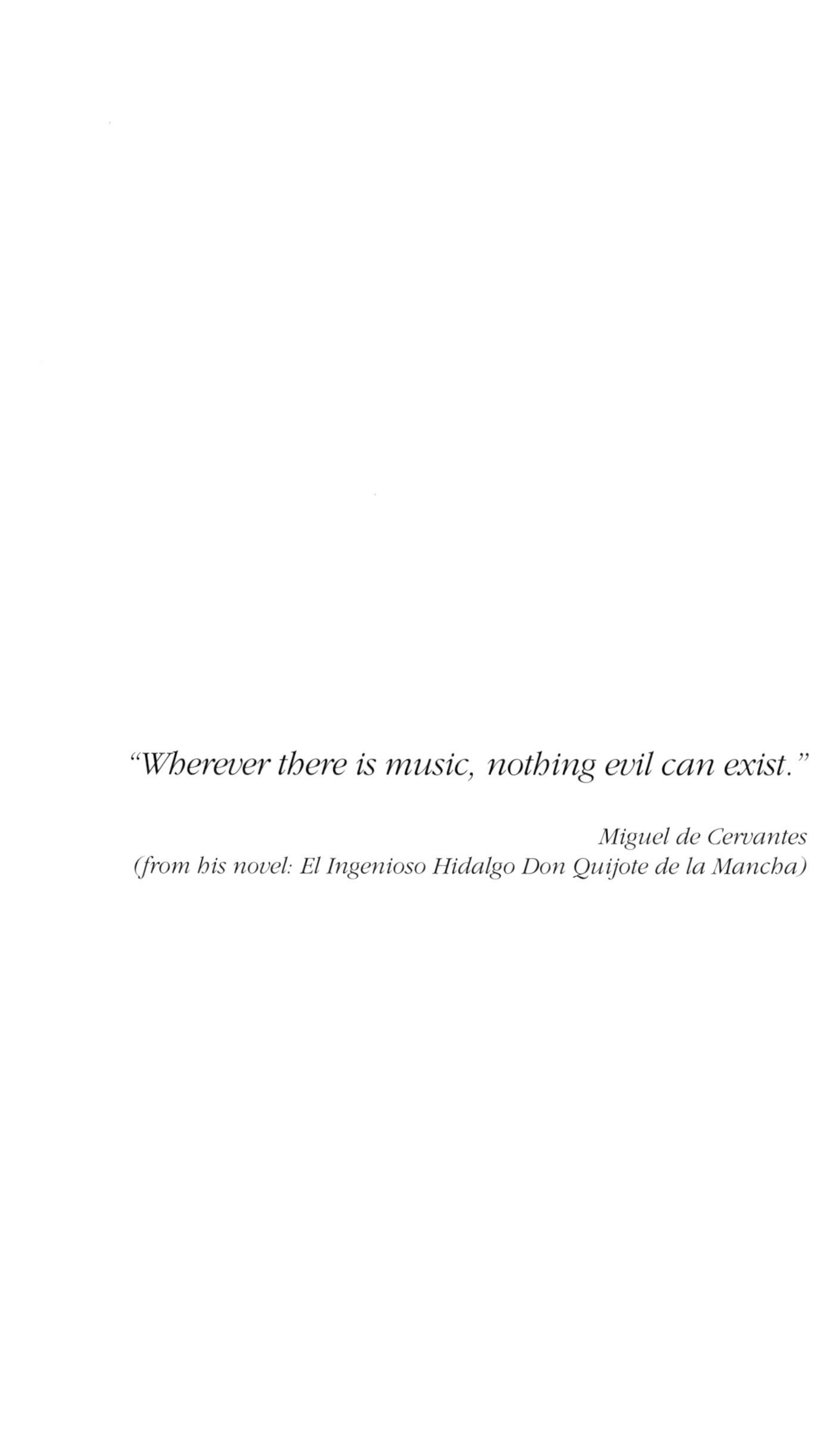

"Wherever there is music, nothing evil can exist."

Miguel de Cervantes
(from his novel: El Ingenioso Hidalgo Don Quijote de la Mancha)

My most sincere gratitude to Lil Guevara and Daniel Salas for their very valuable and enthusiastic collaboration in preparing and publishing this book. It is the summary of a passion that has been with me all my life.

I am also grateful to all my friends that read the Spanish book prior to its publication and contributed their their invaluable suggestions: Yolanda Gómez, Ana María Raga, María Adela Alvarado, Enrique Ribera, Montse Roger, Rima Ibrahim, Liliana Mayz, Miguel Astor, María Leticia González and María Guinand. Thanks also to Flor Martínez, my ever-faithful copyist, who was in charge of copying and designing all the music examples, and to Alicia Martínez, our graphic designer, who was in charge of the design and page layout of the book.

María Leticia González and Cristian Grases provided the initial English translations; Kathy Romey and Sara Mehlenbacher contributed stylistic suggestions and refinements; and the final translations and polishing were done by Joshua Habermann—a monumental task. Finally, Ron Jeffers and María Guinand did the final proofing and editing of the text. To all of these wonderfully talented friends I offer my deepest, heartfelt thanks.

Alberto Grau

Table of Contents

Introduction

Professional calling transforms every musician into a new Orpheus, for music is a language of peace. Alberto Grau, who I have known for many years, has always been a man of peace. Beyond his innate and developed gifts, music has found in him a worthy place to take root. An even-keeled man, he remained calm in his youth despite facing religious and political extremism. He is neither an outsider nor a traditionalist. Even in music he is neither orthodox nor fundamentalist. I used to tell him he was the only person I knew from the "extreme center". He shows no preference for any particular musical language, be it classical, popular, folkloric, etc. "All music is good," says Alberto, "if it achieves the goals for which it was composed."

What is Alberto's nationality? He descends from Catalonian parents and was born in Vich, but he does not make of his Catalonian heritage a source of disagreement, irrationality, pride, or an issue of political or regional nature. The expansive wave of emigration fleeing Franco's government in Spain, a new diaspora not unlike so many that history has come to know, sent him together with his parents towards Venezuelan coasts. There he found what many of us found: a generous and open people, a place where nobody felt like a foreigner, a country in which to grow and develop. And so it was. The gifts that he has received from these splendid and generous inhabitants of this corner of the earth he has returned ten-fold, giving to his adoptive country the best of himself in a spirit of gratitude, responsibility and *bonhomie*. Choral conductor, composer and member of international music juries, Alberto has traveled many paths. In every place he has visited he has left an impression of a human being gifted with a profound spirituality and deep knowledge of his profession.

An Orpheus reborn, Grau has had to confront many types of experiences, always fearlessly facing the most difficult situations head-on, never fearing a hostile audience or a difficult colleague. He enjoys the recognition of colleagues and the many professional invitations he has received.

I have long believed that there is a difference that separates a musician from an artist. A musician has reached a level in performance, composition or conducting and has completed systematic training, possibly in academia. An artist has transcended the above, transforming himself into a communicator of his own ideas and experiences through music. An artist recognizes his connection to society and era, and gives freely of himself, sharing the best of his personality and knowledge. Alberto was a musician when I met him; however I could already recognize in him an emerging artist. In seconds he deciphered expressive difficulties in a piano score with which I had long wrestled. He understood music; he knew that it could not say anything that could be translated into words. Its essence, its semantics, was purely feeling, comprehensible through intuition, not through reason.

Before long he discovered his purpose as a musician. He stopped "thinking with the fingers", turning away from the piano to speak to the universe through choral music. Thus began his career as an artist.

Going beyond the notion of a simple career, Alberto Grau has found a way to blend his work as a conductor and composer in order to communicate his love for creation, his endless desire for peace, and his commitment to work for a fuller, fairer and untroubled world. He has transformed music into an existence that despite the endless problems in contemporary society has not lost its way. "The earth is tired" he says in one of his works, tired of so much impoverishment, of so much absurdity. Music, as an integrating force of reconciliation, has become the *leitmotiv* of his life. For him music is no longer just a profession, but a way of life. Alberto is someone that, by virtue of being neither Catalonian nor Venezuelan, has become a citizen of the world. He is a nomad who cannot be reduced nor labeled. As with Menuhin, his "only brotherhood is with those individuals from the wide world capable of hearing with unfettered ears, whose country is the kingdom of sounds that knows no boundaries"[1].

Now Alberto gives us in book form a sampling of his rich experience as a choral director. Because this text comes from one of the bastions of the choral movement in Venezuela, there is no doubt that it will be a guide for those who wish to follow the path from music, to art, to transcendence. It is an example of Grau as an educator, a role that he has played as a piano teacher, creator of choirs, and jurist for competitions. Each rehearsal is an education, as it is the creation of a choral ensemble, fundraising for an artistic tour and forging a professional reputation as a model of responsibility. This book is a demonstration of Alberto Grau's mastery. Simply and clearly written, with examples of issues that will be encountered by the novice conductor, it is a welcome resource.

Music is a gift; to know it and to love it, a privilege. When one conducts a choral or instrumental ensemble the prerogative is already an achievement. A choral conductor is a creator transforming symbols into sounds in which souls are revealed, transmitting the composer's and artists' present experiences in sounds from other

---

[1] P. Berteaux: Laudatio to Yehudi Menuhin.

times and places. This is possible as an act of faith, not as an artificial attitude; to conduct is to carry out a spiritual function, creating links to authors, performers and audience. Conducting is not an occupation, but rather the beginning of a legend, for a concert is not a show but a sacred ceremony which calls on sound for inspiration. Conducting demands purpose and aptitude. Great conductors are touched by that indescribable spark that comes form genius. What is genius? Talent alone cannot define nor comprehend it. It has something to do with illumination, but also requires great doses of discipline, devotion and sensitivity and expression in any type of repertoire. A good director is the result of many hours of intense effort. This book opens the doors for whoever wants to walk that path, one that in Grau's case is an open highway, without restrictions or boundaries, open to all directions, reconciling all aesthetic languages through music.

Daniel Salas Jiménez

Schola Juvenil de Venezuela, Symphonic Voices Festival, Palladium, Malmö, Suecia, 2008. Conductor: Alberto Grau

Prologue

Every passing day I become more conscious of how difficult it is to communicate our life experiences to others. Nevertheless I would like to think that this book, which I introduce with the intention of helping other choral directors, will be useful to many. Of the teachings shared in the following pages, the most difficult ideas to convey will be, without a doubt, those referring to the human aspects of our profession.

During my long professional life there were moments when I was not able to find the best solution or most appropriate way to address extra-musical problems and situations. Issues relating to funders and supporters, musical and personal growth of singers and staff, programming, and rehearsal scheduling arise every day, and must often be dealt with immediately. The first chapter of this book attempts to address these issues.

The second part, which I consider more interesting and perhaps the best justification for this work, specifically refers to musical techniques and experiences proven by years of work as a mentor of many conductors, who are today established professionals or conductors of multiple choral ensembles from elementary school choirs to professional ensembles.

Throughout my artistic career I have been honored with national and international awards, both in composition and choral conducting. I have been fortunate to be able to study with and get to know great masters, from whom I learned what to do and what to avoid. But when applying these lessons with great humility I understood that sometimes the path must be personal. Convinced by praxis that there are no absolute truths, formulas, or unique method, I still recognize the importance of those who walked the pathways of music before me, and left us their useful precepts. This is why in this essay there will be blended experiences and teachings from masters such as Cristina Vidal de Pereira, Gonzalo Castellanos, Sergiu Celibidache, Carlos Vega, Harriet Serr, Cesar Ferreyra and many others, who on multiple occasions lit the path and inspired me far beyond what they could imagine. To them I address my gratitude in this text which I hope will further their teaching. The following lines, then, are a respectful homage to them, a loving testimony for those who chose to pursue the stimulating path of choral music. These pages are written with the goal of shedding light on the secrets of a profession that is not at all easy, but in a good measure and probably as a result of that difficulty, full of charm and fascination.

Alberto Grau

Great Organ, Inaugural Concert. Main Hall, Centro de Acción Social por la Música, Caracas, Venezuela, 2008. Conductor: María Guinand

Preamble

The Choir from Gabon, an example to reflect upon

> *"Singing is the idealization of the natural
> language of feelings."*

Herbert Spencer [2]

In 2002 I had the honor to participate in the 36th annual *Jornadas de Canto Coral* (Choral Singing Festival) in Barcelona, an event that was successful from both a musical and human standpoint. The morning following the closing ceremony I was in my room ready for departure, when through the window I heard beautiful singing coming from the street. I looked out the window and had the good fortune to observe a choir from Gabon, which had participated in the festival, singing one of the songs in their repertoire. There they were, after an intense week of work and effort, most certainly waiting with their luggage for their bus to pick them up. They had been rehearsing every morning and afternoon, performing in tiring concerts every night in Barcelona and other surrounding cities, yet there they were, radiant and fresh with smiling faces, sharing joy and light through a charming melody and a rhythm rich with old traditions. Their pleasure and desire to continue their music-making was obvious. They sang with love, and I had no doubt that their music was both a comfort and a true spiritual necessity for them. In their voices I heard the sound of an old culture, and despite the unfamiliarity of the language

---

[2] Herbert Spencer (1820-1903). Positivist English philosopher.

and singing style I felt the communication of feelings and emotions common to all people.

I must acknowledge that that unexpected morning concert became one of the musical experiences that I will never forget. Those musicians were following their instincts, their customs, sharing the art they had learned with devotion. They brought with them a beautiful expression of their culture; and through choral singing they gave us an example of what their customs and traditions meant to them. They were returning home, leaving in the pleasant and exotic timbre of their voices more than a memory, a lesson.

I remembered the many ways I had explained to my students the true meaning of music and its value, both aesthetic and human. While listening to this African choir I recalled the occasions I had made the argument to students or colleagues that the only way to create music was to make it flow out of our minds and hearts, that choral music was not "good" or "bad," or that the rendition of a style was not "correct" or "incorrect" because the choral music "popes" said so. Everything had been said by these African voices. It was pointless to get into trivial arguments. They were saying all there was to say with their singing.

Music is a language that connects us through communication and expression. Through music a choir can share values of very diverse communities and eras. Even if we do not understand the meaning of the words, the melodies, harmonies and rhythms reveal to us the perfume of old events, of deep traditions, of times and places long past. Music revives them and makes them ours again. There is no old music; it belongs to the present time. Though science and technology have changed and keep changing very rapidly, human beings are nonetheless human beings. This is why when we read a Greek drama, a picaresque novel, or romantic poetry, when we see the portrait of a renaissance *Madonna* or a wheat field of intense colors and a flock of ravens above it, when we hear a choir of Tibetan monks reciting the sacred syllable in ascending glissandos, or the rendition of the "Gloria" of a solemn baroque mass, or a soprano's love aria, we are touched with an intensity that is equal or even greater that when those works of art were created.

Culture is more than its anthropologic definition. Sometimes it has served to ennoble, sometimes to diminish. Through culture peace has been achieved and conflicts have arisen. Among the great diversity of human cultural achievements music shines as a privileged language. The beauty of its sonorities would be enough, the variety of the combinations of melodies, timbres, rhythms and accompaniments alone would delight us. Yet in the unique possibility of emotion and mutual understanding music offers us still more.

The conductor's responsibility is not limited to the detailed rendition of what is written in the score. The symbols on the paper are only approximations of the ideas that he must confront and clarify through his own spirit. The idea is not to disrespect what is written; on the contrary, the mission is to translate it in order that it be understood and communicated. The academy ennobles, academicism obstructs.

Music-making rests upon the foundation of acquired knowledge that, in order to sustain itself, must be supported by intuition, sensitivity, aesthetics, experience and maturity.

Some conductors value being able to interpret repertoire of the highest technical demands. Others are interested in becoming specialists in the preparation of choral-orchestral works. To achieve these goals, one must start from the beginning, working with easier scores until one can master more complex ones, moving from simpler to more challenging polyphony, acquiring confidence in the performance of greatest variety of repertoire, from the most folkloric to the most academic. Striving to achieve the highest levels of interpretation or becoming a specialist in a particularly difficult repertoire is always laudatory, but only if such a purpose is humbly assumed with perseverance and discipline, progressively obtaining maturity through practice and, most important of all, in the spirit of an enduring love for music.

It is worth highlighting the fact that there is no bad music, just bad musicians, lacking the natural musicality necessary to follow where music leads, thus achieving an ideal interpretation.

The contents of this book move from the general to the specific, from music as a whole to choral music, from the conductor to the choir and the audience, from the rehearsal to the concert. I hope it will be a useful tool of learning for those with the marvelous goal of developing as professional conductors of choirs and orchestras.

The profession of conducting is an unendingly demanding task that is of the utmost service to society. It encourages spiritual and aesthetic growth, and enhances sensitivity and good judgment, making this profession indispensable to our cultural life.

Alberto Grau

Sainte Chapelle Church. Schola Cantorum de Caracas, Paris, France, 1974.
Conductor: Alberto Grau

Petrarca Theater. Schola Cantorum de Caracas, Arezzo, Italy, 1974.
Conductor: Alberto Grau

José Félix Rivas Hall, Teresa Carreño Theater. "Requiem" by Héctor Berlioz, Caracas, Venezuela, 1987. Conductor: Alberto Grau

"Consolidado" Cultural Center. Pequeños Cantores de la Schola Cantorum de Caracas, Caracas, Venezuela, 1992. Conductor: Luimar Arismendi

Chapter 1
Music

What is music?

"Music: the feeling that interrupts and transforms
reason, almost making you lose the sense
of who you are, of where you are.
It is the irrational part of expression."

Federico Nietzsche [3]

"Music? If you define it you destroy it.
It is better to feel it, make it, live it,
without trying to define it.
Words are the tomb of ideas. Music must not be
destroyed by saying what it is, because
that is not it. Music is nothing. It is much,
it is everything, but only so far as is so you
feel it, not when you explain it or talk about it."

Daniel Salas [4]

After reading the heading of this chapter, along with the thoughts of Friedrich Nietzsche and Daniel Salas, I realize it is an arduous task to represent the essence of a language that is not built with words but with sounds that leave imprints in our memory and affect our ideas and aspirations.

I include this chapter in my choral conducting compendium in the hope of abolishing harmful taboos so conductors can freely fulfill their important role with their ensembles and in their communities. Together with their choirs they must honestly and passionately carry out their mission as educators of sensitive artists who serve a larger musical world.

---

[3] Friedrich Nietzsche (1844-1900). German philosopher of noticeable influence in contemporary thinking.
[4] Daniel Salas (1935–) Venezuelan university professor, musicologist, historian and music critic.

Music is a sound tapestry of five dimensions. It spans *time* in duration, its *breadth* is expressed in harmonies and contrapuntal structures. Its *height* is revealed in registers and dynamics, and its *depth* communicates the historical context in which it was conceived: period, style, history, intention of the author, etc. Its *existence* in the present moment includes all of the aforementioned qualities, transmuted into current experience. Emotion gathers all previous culture into a continuous flow of reality and moment-to-moment consciousness. It is an affective communication comprised of voices and instruments whose message is unique to each listener.

In music there is both a tenuous breeze and the coarse winds of war. Its flow can resemble the delicate trickle of water, or a crashing waterfall. A musical score, be it effervescent or transcendent, cannot fully reveal the profound secret of music. Only the sensitivity, intuition and knowledge of the interpreter who clarifies, explains, translates, organizes and makes sense of what is written can give concrete meaning to the mystery of its symbols, facilitating the understanding of its message, and drawing aside the veils that separate us from its contents.

The choir conductor must take on the difficult and beautiful task of making music from a written score. This work is comparable to the creative act of composition. When the thread of music's hidden message emerges from the voices of the choir, the music is reproduced and rewritten, giving it new life. There is in this profession something of the magician's sorcery, of the alchemy of the sorcerer who, like a new King Midas, converts the paper score into golden sound. In music there is no shortage of magic, enchantment and charm.

Much has been written regarding melody, rhythm, harmonic progressions, phrasing, form, aesthetics, etc.

It is not my intention to redefine concepts, but to offer a perspective to enhance the conductor's judgment, musicality, and understanding of text. In ancient times it was thought that sound consisted of regular vibrations, while noise was made of irregular ones. Noise had no place in music except when specifically produced by percussion instruments. Nowadays this concept has changed. The difference between sound and noise is the lack of order and causality in the latter. When noise is rationally organized it can be incorporated into music as sound.

Sincere expression, spiritual openness and surrender to the music are at least as important as technical perfection in a performance. The greatest rigor in the mechanical transmission of what an author has written is worthless if such precision is not accompanied by genuine emotion. As with any language, music is a means of communication. Where a poet uses language to transmit ideas and feelings through words, the interpreter of music must re-create sounds that engender the thoughts and feelings behind the written symbols.

Music is both emotion and reason. Maestro Celibidache[5] often said that the music could happen "while one shaves every morning." Music is also the traditional Catalonian melody sung by my political exile father. Often emotion prevented him from finishing that song that came from the deepest places of his soul. Music can equally be the call to prayer of the muezzin[6] from the minaret, the chanting of a rabbi in the synagogue, or a Gregorian melody vibrantly resonating in a dark Romanesque church. Music is an eager and fervent gospel hymn sung by a group of untrained voices in a

---

[5] Sergiu Celibidache (1912-1996). Romanian orchestra conductor and educator; recognized for his passion for detail, memory, expressiveness and wisdom.

[6] Mohammedan that calls for prayer from the minaret (the tower of the mosque).

small church in the American South. Music is a native song in the Amazonian forest, or the sound produced by an orchestra, or a children's choir which, despite minor technical imperfections, is charged with the energy of those who make music from the depths of their hearts.

Music is a rational product expressed in the musical score, but it is also experience and communication, a transmission of life force in which the musician's feelings and all that has shaped him come together. In order to reach high communicative and expressive levels in the interpretation of the work being studied, a musician requires not only the necessary technical knowledge, but also intelligence and intuition, to reveal the message of the piece and transfer it to the performers.

Music and Life

"We can create, interpret or simply 'hear' music without knowing anything about musical notation. Therefore musical notation is not music."

Carlos Vega[7]

In a musical composition the end is implicit in the beginning. A natural progression towards the final note begins with the first one. This is true of all living things.

In a musical discourse the space between the silence preceding the piece and the silence following it is made up of sounds and pauses that form a musical discourse. From the first sound, the act of perception involves a conscious movement from a quiet, expectant state to one of alert

---

[7] Carlos Vega (1898-1966). Eminent Argentinean musicologist. His contributions to the study of phraseology are still very current and important.

attention. In this attentive state the musician's intuition is engaged and the conductor as a re-creator understands that the composition's flow must be respected, ensuring continuity and coherence. As a written text has commas or semicolons, music has rests and fermatas, long or short, that should not become the equivalent of full stops. For the various soundscapes must follow one upon another, leading inevitably to the true conclusion of the work.

In more extended works (concerto, symphony, mass, oratorio, etc.), pauses between sections should not interrupt natural pacing which the composition requires. Composers, aware of this necessity, often indicate linkage of musical sections through instructions such as *attacca*, or *segue*, or they sometimes compose connecting music. A mass as accompaniment for the religious rite is conveniently fragmented to adapt it to the natural flow of the liturgy, but as a purely musical work, its flow must be maintained, and this requires the proper length for the pauses between sections.

Music as a language

Maestro Cesar Ferreyra[8] writes in his *Cuentos Corales* (Choral Tales)[9]: "Music does not have only two dimensions: length and width; it has a third dimension: depth, and perhaps other dimensions as well: temporal, stylistic, historical, psychological, intentional, etc."

Both science and music create knowledge and deepen our understanding of ourselves and the world around us. Whereas science uses observation, experimentation and induction, the study of musical style recreates the reality

---

[8] Cesar Ferreyra (1926-2001). Maestro and choral conductor of great prestige, born in Cordoba, Argentina.
[9] Ferreyra, Cesar: *Cuentos Corales*. GCC Editions. 1999. Buenos Aires, Argentina.

of the cultural surroundings in which music evolved. Music is therefore a cultural artifact, an achievement of our civilization just as much as any scientific or mechanical invention. Though their methodologies are dissimilar, science and music serve similar ends.

As a language, music has its own phonetics, syntax and semantics. The study of musical language is intellectual, as is the study of art of dance (see Chapter 5.) The final artistic product, however, is the result of talent or genius and other concepts that are difficult to define, catalogue or explain. Among them is the fundamental concept of energy, to which we now turn our attention.

Music and energy

The concept of energy in the sense that we are concerned with comes from the Latin word *virtus*, meaning "efficacy," "power," "capacity to act." Its etymology comes from the Greek energia, implying "willpower," "vigor," "tenacity," and "force capable of transforming itself into physical effort." This term can also imply spiritual, intellectual or physical courage. In these senses energy is the most evident manifestation of life force.

Singing as a soloist or chorister is both spiritual and physical. Before competing, athletes stretch while concentrating on the challenge before them. Similarly, before going on stage, choristers do breathing, intonation, and other "warm-up" exercises and concentrate their thoughts on the artistic experience in which they are about to partake. There is an obvious relationship between sports and choral art. As singer and professor Margot Pares Reyna[10]

---

[10] Margot Pares Reyna. Venezuelan soprano and professor of international reputation.

once pointed out: "a singer is the sportsman of sound." Similarly Vittorio Gassman[11] defined an actor as an "athlete of the soul," and theatrical practice as "the gymnastics of the heart."

In our culture the concept of *anima-animus,* aside from the grammatical genre, represents two sides of our existence. The Romans had Venilia and Selacia: one the goddess of the wave that comes to shore, and the other the goddess of the wave that returned to the sea. Why two goddesses if there was only one wave? If the water that comes and goes is always the same water? The strength and the substance are the same, but the direction and the quality of the energy are different and opposite. *Anima* was the wind, a continuous flow of movement and life. In many cultures, not only in Greece, the human body was likened to a percussion instrument. *Anima* was the beat, the vibration, the rhythm.

Anima can also be recognized in a singer's concentration, the slackening of the singer's facial muscles, and look of complete attention. Choristers, like the *yogis* who transform their bodies into instruments, must care for their voices with the same care and interest. Singers, because they carry their instrument internally, must take care of it, and must know how best to put it to use. This is a matter of continually focusing the vital energy that ultimately music must express. Music is vibrant energy transmitted through sound waves that, upon arriving at the eardrum, is transformed into audible sound. An instrument is required to perceive this energy.

In order to sound properly, a violin needs both the sensitivity and physical energy of the violinist. Likewise, the singing of a madrigal requires energy from the deep,

---

[11] Vittorio Gassman (1922-2000), Famous Italian actor and master of cinema and theater.

personal source where the vocal instrument begins. This instrument is set to motion by the energy given it by singers in conjunction with the anatomical-physiological-mental-spiritual reality of their being. The unique nature of the voice is such that the phonating apparatus both "belongs to the singer," and "is the singer." Practice, experience, serious concentration, and refinement of the vocal instrument are the prerequisites for harnessing this energy effectively.

We focus on this to highlight the reasons why energy must play a vital role in the rehearsal, so that it not become a shallow process, but rather be informed by a methodology involving vocalization, physical preparation, and concentrated study of the repertoire.

Both the master of martial arts and the disciplined practitioner of *hatha-yoga* know that their efforts require a high level of energy. They understand that their mind must be at the service of their body, one solid unit able to achieve maximum agility. The effective combination of tension and relaxation facilitates movement, and allows them to maintain precise positions effortlessly. The body-mind unit is the practitioner's tool.

There is no human activity that does not require energy. The difference between something that is done well and something that is done poorly is often traceable to the way energy is harnessed. If energy is scattered, or we act without concentration, it is unlikely that we will achieve desirable results. There are occasions, of course, when attention is reduced, especially in repetitive, mechanical tasks. Walking or going down the stairs does not require concentrated energy. Simply being attentive enough to avoid falling is enough, for under normal conditions no one takes a step thinking about which muscle to move next.

In the realm of artistic languages, however, directed and coordinated energy yield the best results. A dancer cannot perform a single *plié* without awareness of all the details of the choreography. The same is true for a watercolor painter, because one careless stroke made without concentration can cause irreparable damage to the work. In theater, as Antonio Barba[12] has said, the actor must feel that "all his body is alert, ready, prepared to act in a precise way".

Theater, like music, is an art of time and space. The actor moves across the stage (space) over the course of his various actions (time). Music reaches the ear as a part of the musical discourse (time), as well as through the sounds of the musical language in contrapuntal and harmonic textures, and in formal structures (space). Actors move physically through space to deliver their lines. Some energy is projected, and some is accumulated, conserved for future action. An actor's skill lies in the ability to smoothly manage both the projected and retained energy.

Referring to Konstantin Stanislavski,[13] Vasili Toporkov[14] stated that one must "have the right rhythm," even if one can't define exactly what that means. Stanislavski knew well that a scene could not be presented in a diminished state of alertness. Energy had to be channeled until even the tiniest of details had been perfected. For Stanislavski, theater was about going beyond day-to-day life, and heightening the audience's experience. In this way communication was amplified as the actor reproduced the sensory and emotional world of his character. This required unlimited attention and total energy focused on bringing the audience into the deep truth of the theatrical experience beyond any superficiality.

[12] Antonio Barba. 20th century theater director and anthropologist.
[13] Konstantin Stanislavski (1863-1938). Russian actor and director, creator of the Moscow Art Theater who transformed psychological realism into an interpretation technique.
[14] Vasili Toporkov. Russian theater actor and director in the 19th and 20th centuries.

To "have the proper rhythm" was to create life force, a manifestation of energy. "The right rhythm", said Stanislavski, is "the one that makes you turn your body and hit the mouse that is right behind you in the proper instant, which is different from the rhythm required if what is behind you is a tiger". One must not be inattentive; there is no place for delay in action. Life goes hand in hand with action, and life is vitality and energy. Like the actor, the chorister and conductor must harness this intangible resource of energy.

Similar to the life of yogis on a rug while doing their *asanas*, the master of *chi* on a *tatami*, pole-vaulters preparing their run, the chess champion, or the stage director, the action of a chorister on stage is about energy. One has to know how best to use it, if one hopes to achieve the most satisfactory result. Through the rehearsal process, choir conductors are responsible for this. They are responsible for encouraging each chorister to give their best. During rehearsal this might seem excessively demanding, but as Mei Lanfang[15] said referring to martial arts: "to achieve higher levels, one must start from the bottom and make sacrifices, enduring difficult moments that tire both soul and body. This is the only way to ensure victory at the end."

Success makes one forget the hardships, mistakes, bitter moments, and the energy required in order to not give up. In martial arts, children are pushed to the limit of their capabilities. The weariness, the splinters, the bruises that are products of the early incompetence of the novice sometimes makes it appear that the demands are greater than what they should be. In his autobiography Mei Lanfang asserts that the satisfaction of being able to portray the role of a 60-year old warrior woman was the

---

[15] Mei Lanfang (1895-1961). Maestro and actor of "The Beijing Opera; specialized in feminine roles.

result of the tenacity and the discipline his masters instilled in him during his childhood.

What has been said might appear to be too radical, but the truth is that we need energy, and then more energy, to overcome difficulties and to open up a space for growth in our personal and professional development.

Music Notation

"To define music as the art of combining sounds is to confuse it with its notation. It is almost the same as confusing poetry with the alphabet."

Carlos Vega

"Trying to explain interpretation only through musical notation is a regretful limitation. It is closing your eyes to nature, to the other arts that accompany sound, to life itself."
"Truthful interpretation is kaleidoscopic: unforeseen, unexpected, never repeated, and always new."

César Ferreyra

Inaccuracy of the score

As "musical topography", written music is fixed. However, its interpretation will vary from one interpreter to another. Furthermore, beyond what the score indicates, there is always the search for a complete musical expression, which could sometimes imply working against music's natural tendencies in order to obtain the best artistic result. These alterations should never be the result of whim or the incompetence of the interpreter, but of a thorough study that leads the conductor to conclusions that can be difficult to comprehend. In these cases, intuition plays a fundamental role.

Fidelity to a written composition is frequently cited when demanding that conductor and interpreters do not deviate from the instructions written in the score. Transformed into an unquestioned dogma, this loyalty towards the written score can become a trap that separates us from the best aesthetic and artistic results. Loyalty is sometimes a virtue, but if it is invoked by conductors and interpreters based on rigorous academic prescriptions, it can only be considered arbitrary and inadequate.

Music is not, nor should it be, exactly what is written. On the contrary, the notes are the suggestions, more or less precise symbols, of what the composer was able to notate in signs that can never express the complete feeling of music nor represent with fidelity the last intention of the author. Whereas pitch can be notated with specificity on the staff, other elements cannot be precisely written, so the final decision as to how to interpret these comes from the performers and conductor. This inaccuracy of notation can sometimes deform the logical sense of the musical discourse if it is accepted unquestioningly.

If followed with servility, dynamics written in the score can hamper the emotion and communication that are absolutely necessary to properly interpret the subtleties of music. There follow some examples of misleading notation, in this case regarding the placement of bar lines, in compositions of Johann Sebastian Bach, Jacques Arcadelt, Francisco Guerrero and Miguel Letelier. It is important to reiterate that these potential defects of the works are problems of musical notation, and not of the undoubted genius of the creators of such inspired works.

Aria
Final aria – Motet "Komm, Jesu, Komm" by Johann Sebastian Bach (1685-1750)

Example of a melody wrongly written in 3/4, when it should be written in 4/4.

Il bianco e dolce cigno

Jacobo Arcadelt (c. 1505-1568)

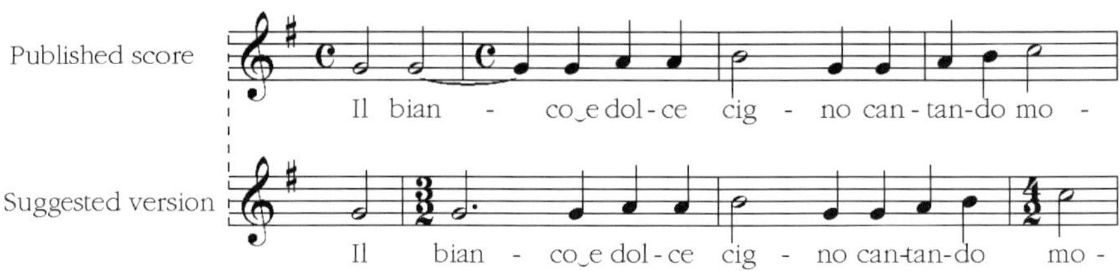

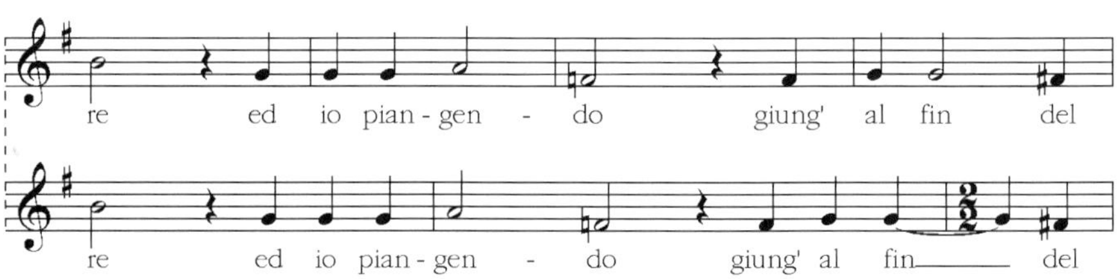

Modification of the placement of the measure lines in accordance with the text.

The white and gentle swan
The white and gentle swan dies singing
and I also cry as I reach the end of my days.

Oh! que nueva
Francisco Guerrero (1527?-1599)

Example of misleading bar lines.

The work of Spanish musicologist Samuel Rubio, which includes a great collection of antique music, is without a doubt admirable; however those first editions of important fifteenth and sixteenth-century Spanish composers deserve new revisions to clarify their music notation.

What great News!
> *What great and happy news*
> *you bring to us!*
> *For the manger in Bethlehem*
> *is now made into paradise.*

Arbolé, arbolé

Lyrics: Federico García Lorca (1898-1936).
Music: Miguel Letelier (Chile, 1939-).
Review and interpretative version: Alberto Grau.

Tree, Tree
dry and green.
The girl with the beautiful face
is picking olives
while the smooth wind of Torres
embraces her waist.

Barlines do not always serve the music, especially in certain works where they are incorrectly written, or in richly contrapuntal pieces in which they can obscure the melodic organization.

Slavishly following what is written in a score without reflection has frequently led to an interpretative tradition that, rather than facilitating the better comprehension of the work, damages it, giving rise to chronic mistakes and misunderstandings requiring constant correction.

It can be useful to know how other conductors and ensembles have interpreted a determined work in order to compare possible ways of revealing its contents, but these should never be taken as definitive models to follow. Conductors must study the score independently from any previous interpretative suggestion in order to extract from it what they consider important, even if this does not match what other noteworthy artists have done.

John White, consultant of *New York Pro Musica,* was once asked if there was a fundamental contradiction in his progressive ideas regarding ornamentation in Monteverdi's music. White answered: "You can do what you want because it will be considered correct; but first go get a doctorate in music in Harvard…"

Intuition in music

*"Intuition? But of course, extremely
important! Its irreversible nature? Time
(whatever this is!) moves (?) forward (?).
There is no turning back. It is not even
necessary, because what is 'behind' is in front
of you."*

Daniel Salas

*"If we mix water and oil in a cup, the oil will
always float on top of the water no matter
how determined we are."*

Sergiu Celibidache

*"If you close the door to all mistakes, you will
never allow truth to come in."*

Rabindranaz Tagore [16]

In the interpretation of a musical score, intuition is as important as reason. Through intuition we often perceive an essential musical message that is inaccessible through the application of pure logic alone.

Based on the development of phenomenology by Edmund Husserl[17], Sergiu Celibidache blended the values of intuition and essence within a concept of conducting, with the purpose of achieving a complete and correct musical expression.

The application of intuition sometimes leads us to consider musical ideas that are contrary to those that would arise from only logical and natural laws. Occasionally

---

[16] Rabindranaz Tagore (1861-1941). Hindu poet; awarded the Nobel Prize in Literature.

[17] Edmund Husserl (1859-1938). German philosopher whose fundamental contribution, phenomenology, is an abstraction method of absolute and transcendental elements that offer a logical meaning to reality.

phenomenological tendencies coincide with natural ones, but at other times they can be opposed. Intuition is capable of sensing intangible forces to which reason has no access, sometimes allowing a more satisfactory resolution of a musical issue. Reality can be presented more clearly through this use of intuition, bringing together phenomenology and Bergsonian[18] irrationality.

According to this, intuition reveals that:

- There is only one optimum tempo for a specific musical moment. It is determined by the influence of elements such as the state of mind of the conductor and musicians, the acoustics of the space, the level of musicianship of the interpreters, and the personalities of the interpreters as they affect expression.
- The relation between one moment and the next can only be known through the continuity of the musical discourse.
- Changes in tempo (pulse, character) follow reason, experience, and especially intuition.
- There is an optimal tempo to correlate the sections of a score. In the wise conductor, knowledge and experience reinforce intuition to determine tempo. The indications of the composer or editor must be reference points, but the conductor must always assume the ultimate responsibility for the interpretation.

Repetition in music

Nothing in life can be repeated. This is evident when we try to relive moments of past happiness. For example, we can hear a good recording of a good concert or see video footage of it, but the emotion is somehow different. New experiences have been accumulated, feelings have

---

[18] Henri Bergson (1859-1941). French philosopher; awarded Nobel Prize. Defender of intuition, he opposed intellectualism and mechanicism.

changed; we can never be exactly as we once were. The event belongs to the past and cannot be modified, or relived as it was.

Is often said, "what is good, when brief, is better." Therefore in music we must avoid mechanical and thoughtless interpretations. It is vital to vary repetitions lest the music suffer. To avoid monotony, intensity or tension must be gained or lost, always giving a different presentation to each appearance of the repeating musical fragment by using small dynamic changes, enhancing any contrapuntal detail, or making subtle variations in time or color. In this way the music is revitalized and imbued with expressive possibilities.

When conductors begin to study a new score in which repetition is present, it is recommended that they be aware, from the outset, of varying expressive paths. Another way to face this interpretative difficulty, which requires more experience from the conductor, is to instantly change the dynamic, tempo, or bring out melodies or rhythms that have not been perceived the first time through. Sometimes one must deal not with one repetition but many, for example in a verse-refrain structure. In this case, if the choir sings from memory and has a clear and responsive relationship with the gesture of the conductor, a great deal of flexibility is possible.

These interpretative choices must always be made with subtlety and care for the poetic character and intention of the piece. Compositions from the Spanish, Italian, French, or Flemish Renaissance can often benefit from this treatment, reacting with freedom to the fine texts upon which many of the works are based. To illustrate what has been said regarding repetition we present *Dindirindin, dindirindin,* an anonymous 16th century composition, with some suggestions for potential modifications

Dindirin, dindirin

Spanish anonymous, sixteenth century
(Published score, Europa Cantat Bulletin)

II Ruyseñor, le ruyseñor, Fácteme aquesta embaxata, Dindirindin.
   Y digaolo a mon ami que ju ja so maritata, Dindirindin.

Dindirin, dindirin

Version suggested by the author with changes of character and notation based on the text

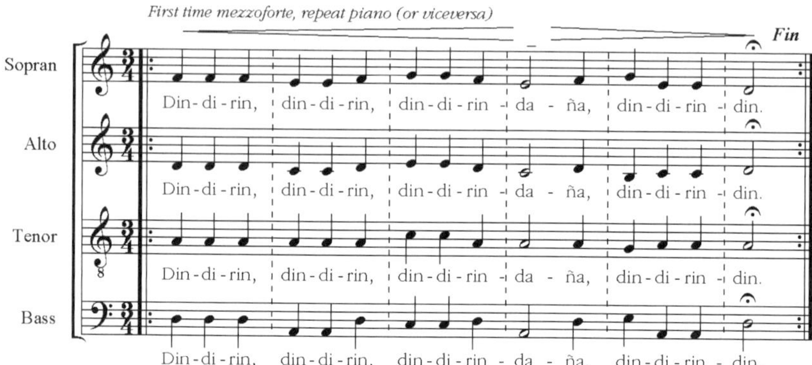

Dindirindin,dindirindaña
  I woke up early on a beautiful morning
  in the plains.
  I found a nightingale
  that was singing on the tree.
  Dindirindin.
  Nightingale, dear nightingale,
  do me this favor:
  tell my friend that I am already married.

When dealing with multiple verses often the placement of the bar lines must be modified for each verse.

Here are some other examples of these practices. We chose a composition of Juan de la Encina (1468-1529) entitled *¡Ay triste que vengo,!* and another piece by fifteenth-century Spanish Renaissance composer Pedro Escobar entitled *Las mis penas madre.*

¡Ay triste que vengo!

Juan de la Encina (1468-1529)
(Published score, Europa Cantat Bulletin 1961)

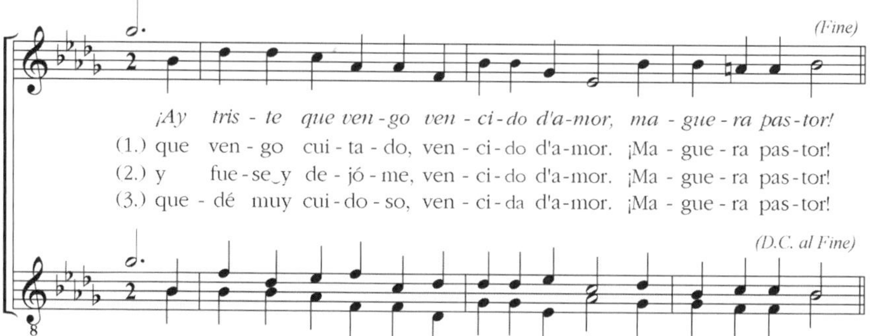

¡Ay triste que vengo!

Version suggested by the author

(1.) que vengo cuitado... - *Un poco más fuerte y acelerando*
(2.) y fuese y dejome... - *Forte y alargando*
(3.) quedé muy cuidoso... - *Poco meno mosso, ralentando y diminuendo*

Oh, how sad I come, / defeated by love. / Good gracious shepherd, / It would be better not to go to the market / so that I will not return so sad. / I come filled, / defeated by love. / With loving eyes I looked at her and she looked at me / and she left and I stayed, defeated by love. / Good gracious shepherd, / Seeing her I am love struck and have no peace or rest, / I am left trembling, defeated by love. / Good gracious shepherd.

Beyond the suggested changes in the meter, additional modifications of tempo and dynamics for each verse can enrich its interpretation. For example: First time *mezzoforte, moderato*; second time *piano, allegretto*; third time *forte, legato amoroso*; and fourth, repeat the first section "Ay triste" *forte, legato e rallentando*.

Las mis penas madre
Pedro Escobar (1465-1535)
(Published score, Europa Cantat Bulletin)

My regrets, mother, are because of love.
Come out, my Lady,
said the orange tree,
because you are so gracious
that even the air will love you.

In this piece it is important to vary tempo and intensity, for example: first verse *piano, in tempo* and *poco crescendo*; second verse *poco affretando* and with more intensity; third verse *poco meno mosso, suplicante*; fourth lyrics *poco più forte* and *intense*; and fifth verse *amoroso, allargando, ritenuto e piano*.

Sometimes it will be suitable to skip a repetition written in the score. This is more likely in early music where formally repeating structures are the rule. Rigorously respecting all the repetitions might have been appropriate in the period when these pieces were composed, but nowadays these reiterations generate weariness in the audience and are not always musically justifiable. In present times interest in maintaining the "purity" of the written score is more of an archeological urge than a musical need. This is not to say that in good musicians may not choose to perform a piece with all its repetitions, or use period instruments, but it is a false conclusion to think that these are the only valid renditions, or that they represent more accurately the musical thinking of the composers.

All music is good

Music theorists have long struggled in their attempts to delineate the criteria by which one can objectively evaluate the quality of music. It may prove beneficial to adopt this aphorism: "All music is good". I have believed this for years, and I have yet to find an exception.

It is true that a piece can be written or interpreted in a better or worse way, or that one can find an audience that is more or less sensitive or receptive, but this is a question of other elements that are related to the talent and intelligence of the composer, the interpreters that are delivering the piece, and also the audience to which the message is projected. Without a doubt, not even the most devout follower of formalistic aesthetics can deny that all music generates emotions, ranging from total boredom to sublime and transcendental exaltation. What we feel while listening to a musical work is related to our culture and personal taste. For instance, a piece that moved us in our adolescence could prove less interesting in our adult life, or vice-versa, but being impassive in regards to music is unthinkable. As Shakespeare[19] wrote in *Merchant of Venice*, the souls of those not moved by music are black as hell.

A language is good insofar as it is communicates, and I see no reason that this would not apply similarly to music. Its complexity, expressed for example in its multiplicity of timbres or polyphony, only enriches its communicative power. If the musical message is properly conveyed, either what the composer intended or what the listener perceived, then it is enough.

I think it is wrong to confine music to hierarchies or to categorize it as academic, popular or folkloric. These are classifications that I accept only for pedagogical purposes, and only when it is clear that music is a unique and indivisible language, whether it be a Haydn symphony[20], a *bolero* of Agustín Lara[21], or the chanted *Bhayángs*[22] of a Hindu dervish.

All music is good, even if that quality is obscured by a poor interpreter. Sometimes the deficiency of a piece is due to a lack of inspiration. No matter how skillful a composer's use of language, if he has nothing of interest to communicate we are left cold. I am reminded of a quip by Oscar Wilde:[23] "he has nothing to say, but he says it in a charming way."

A composer will only be a relevant artist when his scores become something more than sonic rambling

---

[19] William Shakespeare (1564-1616). Dramatist and poet; leading figure of English literature.

[20] Joseph Haydn (1732-1809). Noteworthy Austrian composer of the classical period.

[21] Agustín Lara (1900-1970). Famous Mexican singer and composer of the 20th century.

[22] Bhayángs. Traditional Hindu chant.

[23] Oscar Wilde (1856-1924). Noteworthy English poet, novelist and dramatist.

without sense or order. When music fails to communicate, the defect is always either in the interpreter or the composer, but never in music itself. Music can only follow the laws of nature, which are often altered by "civilized man" who reacts in an intellectual way, preferring that quality to his intuitive and spiritual capabilities.

The purposes for which music is composed are unending. The quality of music is found not only within the composition itself which could be the product of a single composer or, in the case of an oral tradition, the collaboration of an entire community, but also in the relationship between the work and the larger communicative purpose for which it was created.

Orfeón Universitario Simón Bolívar, Choir Olympics, Linz, Austria, 2000.
Conductor: María Guinand

Chapter 2
Music as a fluid

Music flows in time, but every sound that reaches us does so in the present instant. The listener will "organize" it in his mind in relation to the sounds already perceived in order to untangle the sense of the whole. Based on perception of musical flow the conductor must take the following into consideration:

1. Because the natural tendency of a repeated sound is to generate less tension, the creator (composer or interpreter) will in some cases have to account for this to facilitate a better transmission of the message.

Natural tendency

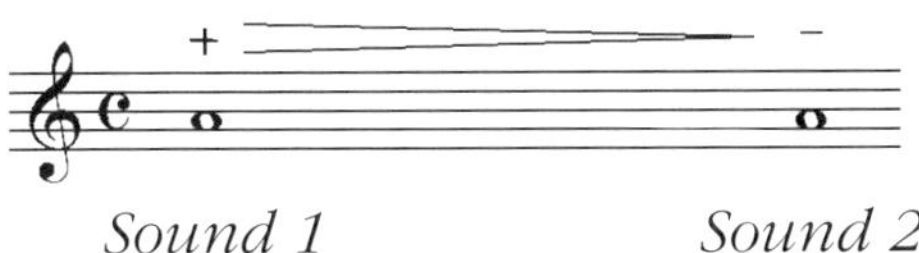

Inverse tendency

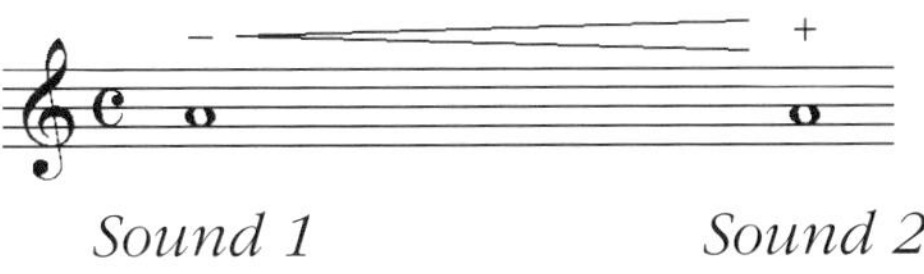

2. Higher sounds generate greater tension, and vice versa.

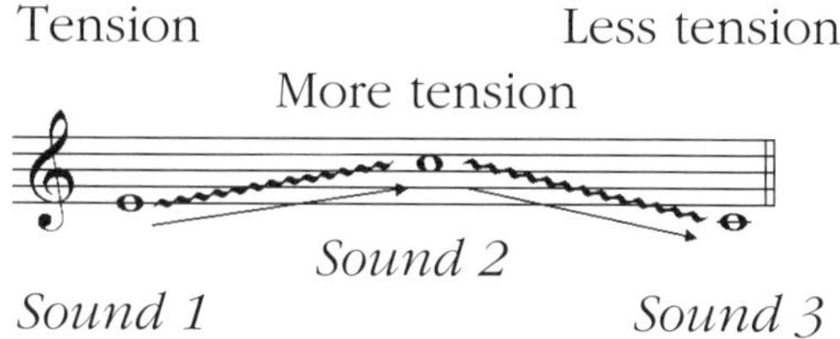

3. A descending melody naturally tends to resolve to the fundamental of its key (tonic).
4. From a melodic and harmonic point of view, there are crucial moments in every piece:
   - Beginning
   - Climatic points
   - Profound points
   - Ending.

It has already been established in physics that every mass set to motion by external forces has the natural tendency to return to its state of rest (Max Plank[24]). From an acoustic point of view, music can be studied within those same physical principles. Philosophy and psychology have contributed to an awareness of the link between the acoustic event and its perception as a consequence of the reflexes of human conscience. Before hearing a sound, acoustic perception is in an "amorphous" state. Awareness of sound awakens it from that condition, generating an expectation of sounds to follow.

The laws that control music are similar to those of fluid mechanics. Like water, a melody flows horizontally, moving forward and relaxing in turn. As Maestro Carlos Alberto Pinto Fonseca[25] has poetically expressed: "Music

---

[24] Max Plank (1858-1947). Physics Nobel Prize. His theories were the bases for quantum and moderns physics.
[25] Carlos Alberto Pinto Fonseca (1933-2007). Brazilian Maestro, composer and conductor.

is like a river, in some occasions running tumultuously between steep cliffs, and others flowing easily between broad banks. When the water encounters obstacles, it generates tension, which is then overcome when the accumulated pressure is too great. In music, rhythm and harmony are the elements that propel the melodic fluid creating tension and release."

The study of musical flow, and of the tendency of sound to generate particular sensory reactions, must be carefully considered by the choral conductor. Psychology warns us that extra-musical elements can also influence the listener, altering one's natural reactions. Various factors (state of mind, etc.) can predispose the listener to varying aesthetic conclusions.

The reaction of consciousness to the flow of sound may lead us, for example, to prefer the interpretation of a piece by a particular musician. Certainly this preference is not unreasonable in that it reflects a connection between the sound expressed by the artist and our own intuitive sense of how the piece should flow.

In all music there are tendencies that we could call "natural" because they seem to follow commonly accepted acoustic laws. There are, however, other aspects that are opposed, or "irrational" that can occur in a particular phrase, motive, cadence, or melody. These apparently contrary tendencies have drawn particular interest from those philosophers who are proponents of newer currents and schools of thought.

From the mid-twentieth century some maestros such as Ernest Ansermet[26] and Sergiu Celibidache used the

---

[26] Ernest Ansermet (1883-1969). Swiss orchestra conductor.

expression "phenomenology." They were referring to the study of the link between the first sound perceived (which they named "phenomenon" after Kant[27] and Husserl) and the rest of the subtle and complex flow of music, with its diverse harmonic and melodic progressions and relations between sounds and silence.

They tried to explain perception from a perspective in which not only objective, rational elements were considered, but also those that could only be perceived and comprehended intuitively. They explored human conscience and spirituality, and the different reactions that the interpretation of a musical score could generate in different listeners.

The observations and suggestions that this group of artists set forth are still very current for the choral conductor. The musical aspects that make up a score have inherent qualities that the conductor must harness, taking as a point of departure the text, which has its own particular demands of emphasis, agogic accent, etc. The conductor must also consider the "mandatory" impulse to move towards a determined tonal center. These factors might require the conductor, for example, to modify the resolution of a cadence, or, in other situations, clarify the meaning of a piece by suggesting appropriate priority to the text or the purely musical elements.

It is then valid to ask: Can expressive capabilities be developed in an artist? Is there a system or method that facilitates this? We know that with continuous practice we can learn how to interpret highly technically complex compositions and even phrase them correctly and use appropriate dynamics. But the element that is most important is communication, which can only be achieved through careful study, understanding of all the elements

---

[27] Emmanuel Kant (1724-1894). German philosopher, who reconciles and synthesizes the basic principles of cause/effect, time/space, rationalism and empirism.

of the poetic and musical language and their relationship, intuition, diligent work, professional experience, and the human and personal maturity and sensitivity of the conductor.

Miguel Astor[28] has made an important contribution to the study of musical language with his book entitled *Aproximación fenomenológica a la obra musical de Gonzalo Castellanos Yumar*[29] *(Phenomenological approach to the music of Gonzalo Castellanos Yumar)*, from which we extract the following thoughts of great artists concerning "music as a fluid," and the study of phenomenology:

From Sergiu Celibidache, remarkable Romanian orchestra conductor, thinker and educator of many generations of conductors:

1. a) Music is nothing, any sound could be transformed into music.
   b) The ending must be contained in the beginning, and the beginning in the ending.
   c) Music lives in the eternal present, constantly reinventing itself in the timeless moment.
   d) I am here because I am not here.
2. Music cannot exist without sounds, but a static existence is impossible for music. Thus it is impossible to define what music is. Sound can become music, but this does not mean that we can define what music is. Music appears, and eventually disappears, without ever achieving existence.
3. What is the relation between two notes, where one follows the other? Perhaps the second note is equal

---

[28] Miguel Astor (1958-). Venezuelan musicologist and composer.
[29] Miguel Astor. *Aproximación fenomenológica a la obra musical de Gonzalo Castellanos Yumar.* Ediciones de la Universidad Central de Venezuela. 2002. Caracas, Venezuela.

to the first one, in which case the opposition of two equal notes requires the organizing principle of time. This is the most basic pre-condition for the metamorphosis of all sound into music. Concerning the second note that is physically equal to the first: Does it feel the same? Of course not, because the first note left something; if not, we could not say that the second note is the second one. The second sound has been deprived of the advantage of happening in virgin territory. Instead it happens in a realm that has been informed by the first sound. Does this mean that there are no repetitions in music? Certainly not. The first time I hear something, I receive something; so the second time, which we call repetition, lands in a field that has already been planted. How many times can you step on the same fresh snow? Only once.

4. The relationship between the present, past, and future can be the basis for feelings and emotions that appear in the affective world. Missing a loved one relates to the past. Waiting with disappointment for something that cannot come relates to past and future. Hope is related to the future, repentance to the past and the future, etc. In our affective world there is nothing that fails to relate in a multifaceted way to the experience of time.

5. Time as an object, as it is considered by the idiots who write "eighth note=72" in their scores, does not exist. Time is the condition that allows my conscience to employ its inherent capacity to reduce the multiplicity of phenomena by transforming them into a complex whole.

Two thoughts by Ernest Ansermet, noteworthy Swiss orchestra conductor and founder of the orchestras of Buenos Aires and the *Suisse Romande*:

1. Music can only be tonal, or even polytonal, but never atonal for fear of losing its meaning.

2. The interpreter never finds in his score more than a plan of the motoric actions to be produced. He must always look beyond those notes and, at the end, he never plays what is written, even if he does not play anything that is not in accordance with what is written.

An idea from Gonzalo Castellanos Yumar[30]: "Melody is harmony stripped of its potential; it is horizontal fluid. Harmony is potential, vertical pressure. The intervals that integrate these two aspects move towards resolution of the dialectic inherent in them, demanding a release in proportion with the greater or lesser levels of tension generated."

Finally, a statement by Miguel Astor: "How does one know when a *ritardando* starts or how long a *crescendo* should last, or what is the most appropriate phrasing for a determined musical structure? What is the adequate *tempo* for a music section? How does one "make" music? Often musicians learn intuitively how to shape phrases and how to resolve interpretative issues. Intuition as a valid method to obtain knowledge is gaining acceptance, even in scientific fields."

After all these interesting observations regarding *music as a fluid*, full of brilliant thoughts made by very educated musicians, all of whom are passionately dedicated to the search for truth, we can only repeat those words by Maestro Daniel Salas: "Music? If you define it you destroy it. It is better to feel it, make it, live it, without caring to define it. Language kills ideas. Music must not be destroyed by saying what it is because words cannot capture it. Music is nothing. It is much, it is everything, but always

---

[30] Gonzalo Castellanos Yumar (1926-   ). Noteworthy Venezuelan director, orchestra conductor and conducting professor.

in the proportion that it is felt, rather than explained it or discussed." An additional thought of Celibidache: "Music should not be simply beautiful, but especially true in its emotional message, and in its poignant communicative mission."

If there is anything that distinguishes humans from all other animal species, it is the unending need to discover the reason for everything that exists. This impulse leads one to question and admire an unarguably perfect dawn, or how a horrible fire can be so incredibly beautiful.

For the rest of our lives, as long as the world remains as it has been, we will passionately continue to search out the great mysteries of music, which, like a religion, integrates life and nourishes our bodies and souls as does the air that we continuously breathe. It would be very difficult for someone to become an effective leader in any specialty without the desire to discover the mysteries that form the underpinning of the larger cosmos. The choral conductor who, despite talent and academic studies, does not deeply examine the constant and essential flow of even the simplest of musical structures will not completely achieve the goal of making the message of the music flower in its fullest form.

To illustrate a practical method of analyzing a piece in relation to its natural flow, we present this beautiful work by North American composer Randall Thompson (1899-1984) with some editorial suggestions.

To the Berkshire Music Center
(1940)
ALLELUIA
Author: Randall Thompson
Revision and interpretative version:
Alberto Grau
Original version
Lento
ppp
pp
Al - le - lu - ia al - le - lu - ia al - le - lu - ia al - le - lu - ia al - le
Beginning
Lento
ppp
Sopran
pp
Al - le - lu - ia al - le - lu - ia al - le - lu - ia al - le - lu - ia al - le
Alto
ppp
pp
Al - le - lu - ia al - le - lu - ia al - le - lu - ia al - le - lu - ia al - le
Tenor
ppp
pp
Al - le - lu - ia al - le - lu - ia al - le - lu - ia al - le - lu - ia al - le
Bass
ppp
pp
Al - le - lu - ia al - le - lu - ia al - le - lu - ia al - le - lu - ia al - le
pp
pp
pp
pp dolcissimo
lu - ia al - le - lu - ia al - le - lu - ia al - le - lu - ia al - le
4
p
sempre pp
First Apex moving towards first
lu - ia al - le - lu - ia al - le - lu - ia al - le - lu - ia al - le
p
lu - ia al - le - lu - ia al - le - lu - ia al - le - lu
p
sempre pp
lu - ia al - le - lu - ia al - le - lu - ia al - le - lu
p
sempre pp
lu - ia al - le - lu - ia al - le - lu - ia
p
lu - ia al - le - lu - ia al - le - lu
low point
diminuendo
8
lu - ia al - le - lu - ia al - le - lu
ia al - le - lu - ia
al - le - lu - ia al - le - lu - ia

pp
ia
Low Point
Poco più mosso
al - le - lu - ia
pp
al - le - lu - ia
Beginning of ascent towards new apex
pp
ia
al - le - lu - ia
al - le - lu - ia
pp
mp
al - le - lu - ia al - le - lu - ia al - le - lu - ia al - le - lu - ia al - le - lu - ia al - le
pp
mp
al - le - lu - ia al - le - lu - ia al - le - lu - ia al - le - lu - ia al - le - lu - ia al - le
pp
mp
al - le - lu - ia al - le - lu - ia al - le - lu - ia al - le - lu - ia al - le - lu - ia al - le
pp
al - le - lu - ia al - le - lu - ia al - le - lu - ia al - le - lu - ia
pp
p
pp
p
Beginning of descent towards low point
al - le - lu - ia al - le - lu - ia al - le - lu - ia al - le - lu - ia
Leading voice
lu - ia al - le - lu - ia al - le - lu - ia al - le - lu - ia al - le
lu - ia al - le - lu - ia al - le - lu - ia al - le - lu - ia
lu - ia al - le - lu - ia al - le - lu - ia
pp
p
pp
p dim.
al - le - lu - ia al - le lu - ia
al - le - lu - ia al - le lu - ia
lu - ia al - le lu - ia
al - le - lu - ia al - le lu - ia
al - le - lu - ia al - le lu - ia

pp
al - le - lu - ia al - le - lu - ia al - le - lu - ia al - le - lu - ia al - le - lu - ia al - le -
Area beginning to move towards second apex
Poco più mosso
poco a poco cresc.
più forte
al - le - lu - ia al - le - lu - ia al - le - lu - ia al - le - lu - ia al - le - lu - ia al - le -
più forte
ia al - le - lu - ia al - le - lu - ia al - le - lu - ia al - le - lu - ia
poco a poco cresc.
al - le - lu - ia al - le - lu - ia al - le - lu - ia al - le - lu - ia al - le -
poco a poco cresc.
al - le - lu - ia al - le - lu - ia al - le - lu - ia al - le - lu - ia
p cresc.
mf dolce
lu - ia al - le - lu - ia al - le - lu - ia al - le - lu -
Second Apex
mf
allargando
f
lu - ia al - le - lu - ia al - le - lu - ia al - le - lu - ia
mf
allargando
f
al - le - lu - ia al - le - lu - ia al - le - lu ia
allargando
mf
f
lu - ia al - le - lu - ia al - le - lu - ia al - le - lu
al - le - lu - ia al - le - lu - ia al - le -
mp dim.
p
ia al - le - lu - ia al - le - lu - ia
Poco meno mosso
affretando
p sub.
ia al - le - lu - ia al - le - lu - ia
affretando
al - le - lu - ia al - le - lu - ia al - le - lu - ia
affretando
ia al - le - lu - ia al - le - lu - ia
affretando
lu - ia al - le - lu - ia al - le - lu - ia

poco rall.
a tempo, sostenuto
mp
mp dim.
pp
al - le - lu - ia al - le -
Towards a new low point
Low Point
Moving towards new climax point
allargando
a tempo, sostenuto
mf
pp
al - le - lu - ia al - le -
allargando
a tempo, sostenuto
mf
pp
al - le - lu - ia al - le - lu - ia
allargando
a tempo, sostenuto
mf
pp
al - le - lu - ia al - le - lu - ia
agógico poco rall.
al - le - lu - ia
poco cresc.
mf
pp súbito
lu - ia al - le - lu - ia al - le - lu - ia al - le - lu - ia al - le -
Continues towards the apex
poco cresc.
mf
p súb.
lu - ia al - le - lu - ia al - le - lu - ia al - le - lu - ia al - le -
poco cresc.
mf
p súb.
al - le - lu - ia al - le - lu - ia al - le - lu - ia al - le - lu - ia al - le - lu - ia al - le - lu - ia
poco cresc.
mf
p súb.
al - le - lu - ia al - le - lu - ia al - le - lu - ia al - le - lu - ia al - le - lu - ia al - le - lu - ia
poco cresc.
mf
p súb.
al - le - lu - ia al - le - lu - ia al - le - lu - ia al - le - lu - ia
cresc. poco a poco
mf
lu - ia al - le - lu - ia al - le - lu - ia al - le -
poco a poco cresc.
mf cresc.
lu - ia al - le - lu - ia al - le - lu - ia al - le -
poco a poco cresc.
mf cresc.
al - le - lu - ia al - le - lu - ia al - le - lu - ia al - le - lu - ia
poco a poco cresc.
mf cresc.
al - le - lu - ia al - le - lu - ia al - le - lu - ia al - le - lu - ia
poco a poco cresc.
mf cresc.
al - le - lu - ia al - le - lu - ia al - le - lu - ia al - le - lu - ia

f cresc.
lu - ia al - le - lu - ia al - le - lu - ia al - le - lu - ia al - le -
48
Più forte
lu - ia al - le - lu - ia al - le - lu - ia al - le - lu - ia al - le -
al - le - lu - ia al - le - lu - ia al - le - lu - ia al - le - lu - ia al - le -
al - le - lu - ia al - le - lu - ia al - le - lu - ia al - le -
al - le - lu - ia al - le - lu - ia al - le - lu - ia al - le - lu - ia
Movendo
sfz
lu - ia al - le - lu - ia al - le - lu - ia al - le -
Area of main apex phrase
52
f
movendo mf cresc.
lu - ia al - le - lu - ia al - le - lu - ia al - le -
f mf movendo
lu - ia al - le - lu - ia al - le - lu - ia al - le -
f movendo
lu - ia al - le - lu - ia al - le - lu - ia al - le - lu - ia
movendo
al - le - lu - ia al - le - lu - ia al - le - lu - ia al - le - lu - ia al - le -
stringendo
rall.
lu - ia al - le - lu - ia al - le - lu - ia al - le - lu - ia al - le - lu - ia al - le -
Highest concentration of
56
f cresc. molto stringendo
allargando
lu - ia al - le - lu - ia al - le - lu - ia al - le - lu - ia al - le - lu - ia al - le -
f cresc. molto stringendo allargando
lu - ia al - le - lu - ia al - le - lu - ia al - le - lu - ia al - le - lu - ia al - le -
f cresc. molto stringendo allargando
al - le - lu - ia al - le - lu - ia al - le - lu - ia
f cresc. molto stringendo allargando
lu - ia al - le - lu - ia al - le - lu - ia al - le - lu - ia al - le - lu - ia al - le -

Largamente
intensity and dynamic energy
A tempo
Towards low point
Area of low point
Meno mosso
Lento
Towards the end
End
al niente

Rios Reyna Hall, Teresa Carreño Theater. L. van Beethoven's Symphony No. 9, Caracas, Venezuela, 1997. Conductor: Gregory Carreño

José Félix Ribas Hall, Teresa Carreño Theater. Rehearsal, Caracas, Venezuela, 1988. Conductor: Krzysztof Penderecki

Aula Magna, UCV. Common Song, Caracas, Venezuela, 1980. Conductor: Michel Eustache

Aula Magna Hall, U.C.V. La Doncella, 2007

Schola Cantorum de Venezuela, Barbican Center, London, England 2007.
A Flowering Tree by John Adams.

The Conductor's Leadership

Overview

*"Some basic advice to conductors
(I hardly ever practice it): when you make
religious music, pray!"*

César Ferreyra

*"An orchestra conductor is admittedly
also a theatrical director. He is also an actor
among actors, and a cast member
of a special kind. The orchestra conductor
has a physical and personal connection
with his actors, that is to say,
with the musicians, but above all, with each
specific moment inherent in the music."*

Vittorio Gassman

It doesn't matter whether the conductor is a choral conductor or an orchestral conductor; their responsibility is the same: to communicate to an audience the musical message contained within the boundaries of the score. As this text has been conceived simply for conductors without reference to a choral or orchestral specialization, many of the elements discussed will serve in either circumstance. However, the reader will notice that there are more references to choral conducting.

Choral singers and instrumentalists often approach music from dissimilar backgrounds. Most commonly this is due to the differing natures of choral and instrumental training. Relative to the instrumentalist, who most likely has many years of training, the chorister is more often an amateur, someone who loves music but may have little professional training. In some instances the chorister may even be musically "illiterate". This is not necessarily the case, especially where choral music is part of an academic curriculum and choral singers are well-trained musicians.

Still, these two realities coexist and result in a situation in which choral and orchestral directors call upon different skills to achieve a similar goal.

Choral conducting is further distinguished from orchestral conducting in that the chorister's instrument is built-in. It belongs, personally and physically, to the singer and therefore requires different handling than an instrument that is carried in its case to rehearsals and concerts. This fact is well known by choral conductors and is reflected in their approach.

It is the task of the director to understand each and every one of the sonorous, syntactic and semantic elements in the score, and the relationship between them. In addition to understanding the musical language, directors must be able to transmit their thoughts to the choristers such that the message written by the composer and recreated by the conductor is communicated through the choir to the audience.

In addition to the technical understanding and communicative skill required to be effective, conductors must also remember that in every rehearsal and concert they must be fully expressive. Only through complete emotional engagement by conductor and performers alike can the truth of the work be fully communicated.

Being a good conductor requires both physical and mental preparation. Getting sufficient rest is a basic requirement for avoiding fatigue, which can be a serious detriment to rehearsal or performance. Conducting requires a physical effort that can only be undertaken by one who has created an appropriate program of physical activity and carries it out with discipline. Not only is muscular strength needed, but mental strength is just as indispensable, and the conductor will surely call upon it when physical exhaustion threatens to overcome conductor or choir. A well-trained mind can help to push back fatigue and open new possibilities for deeper music-making.

Control of body and mind, discipline, unwavering focus, sense of humor, and affability—all these are characteristics that the director should have. Fatigue should completely disappear at the moment a rehearsal or concert begins, no matter how much activity and effort has taken place during the day. The ability to overcome it should be instantaneous; it is the product of an act of will that the conductor must demonstrate, and also teach to the members of the choir.

To begin a rehearsal or concert, both conductor and choir should be in the best possible mental and physical state. Only then will the artistic engagement of all performers be satisfactory. As with any challenging activity, previous preparation must take place to achieve the point of readiness. A dancer would not go on stage without doing warm-ups, and the same is true of an athlete. A martial artist, in addition preparing the muscles to react quickly, practices exercises for mental control, concentration, relaxation and liberation from fear. The conductor and members of the choir (or orchestra) should not go on stage or start a rehearsal under the weight of personal worry, chronic fatigue, or any other preoccupation. At the moment the physical warm-ups and vocalizations start the choristers and their leader should live only in the present moment with full intensity.

It is the responsibility of the conductor not only to prepare the choir emotionally, but also physically with an appropriate work-out of breathing exercises, vocalizations and any other type of exercise required to relax the muscles and eliminate unwanted tension. This preparation is vital in achieving focus in the singers and also raising their spirits so that they are filled with energy.

To achieve optimal results, the conductor must attend to the following elements:

- If the choral group is not very experienced, the conductor should select appropriate repertoire, starting with pieces that are easy but attractive to choristers and audience (popular music), or *a cappella* repertoire with few challenges of tessitura and counterpoint.
- The conductor must always have all the material appropriately studied before every rehearsal.
- It is unwise to forget that the concert must always be attractive to both the audience and the choir. Repertoire must contain unity that will make it coherent, but with enough variety that it not cause boredom in the choir or audience.
- The conductor must always try to achieve optimal results in each performance, keeping in mind that music always demands study and many rehearsals in order to achieve satisfactory artistic goals.
- The conductor should know that a concert is both an auditory and a visual experience. The academic tradition of the static and rigid choir is progressively yielding to the incorporation of movement. Some pieces invite subtle movement, while others call for the choir to participate with clapping, stomping, or complex choreography.
- The conductor should use many clear metaphors in rehearsals, inviting the choristers to use imagination and intuition in pursuit of the ever-changing interpretive possibilities that the score offers. All choral music can be compared to the flowing of air, be it a refreshing and serene breeze, sustained wind, unleashed hurricane, or the murmur of the sea.

Character

The conductor's gesture, personality, character, temperament, and physical presence are all important elements that will determine, in one way or another, success. It is not enough to have achieved good grades in music classes, workshops, or seminars specific to choral conducting in order to be a good director. Knowledge is without a doubt indispensable, but cannot itself ensure the professional achievement that characterizes successful conductors.

A choral director works with human beings, who, in addition to being themselves the instruments, also possess peculiarities in their personalities. Everyone who leads groups should know how to work with a team. One must be compliant when appropriate, but also able to uphold standards when the discipline of the group or the interpretative quality is at risk. Conductors must remember that they are seen from the front by the performers, and also from the back by the audience. During performances professional behavior, poise and elegance are essential.

The conductor must be cheerful, but serious in focusing the energy for a good rehearsal. One must be willing to answer any type of question and always maintain a level of camaraderie with all members of the group without compromising leadership. The conductor must always encourage an attitude of openness regarding any suggestion, but must be firm and persuasive when appropriate.

Creativity

> *"It is also necessary to know the rules
> in order to break them. But one must do
> so consciously, with knowledge,
> and not from ignorance."*
>
> *Vittorio Gassman*

> *"Unthinking loyalty is a quality,
> sometimes a virtue, most often associated
> with dogs. We need not subjugate
> ourselves to it, especially if it means
> invoking a prescriptive academic approach
> in the name of authenticity."*
>
> *César Ferreyra*

Pablo Casals[31] said that whereas notes on a page are like a straightjacket, music, like life itself, is constant movement, continuous spontaneity free from restrictions. In this spirit all musical interpretation must be full of creative energy, of unprecedented sensitivity.

"True musical interpretation," says maestro César Ferreyra, "must be kaleidoscopic, that is to say spontaneous, never repeated, always new. No matter how many times a work has been studied or played, we must reflect deeply upon it before presenting it in concert." In this regard, Gassman said: "One must follow the road which is set by the structure of the piece to be played. But this pathway can and must vary, where possible, in order to avoid the routine and the mechanical..."

When we return to a familiar piece the score can appear to be unchanged, but since the previous performance

---

[31] Pau Casals (1876-1973). Famous composer and cellist from Catalonia (Spain). One of his major contributions to music was reviving the cello works of Johann Sebastian Bach and instilling in each one of them a profound aesthetic and spiritual sense.

the conductor will have grown in experience, maturity, sensitivity and artistic depth. No two things are identical, nor should two interpretations of the same piece be the same. On this topic Gassman said: "Every rendition is, to a certain extent, partial in the sense that it enhances certain aspects, images, meanings of the text, and leaves others in shadow." That same premise can be applied to musical interpretation. Each new rendition should demonstrate the growth of the director and the ensemble.

A conductor that cannot improve upon previous performances suffers from:
- a lack of self-critique
- conformism
- insufficient study
- lack of ambition
- insufficient faith in the ensemble.

Preparation of the novice conductor

Beginning conductors, working with children or youth choirs, should set goals that are attainable through sincere effort. In order to help young singers to apply themselves wholly, the conductor must demonstrate with clear examples the best way to interpret a musical passage, instilling in the singers the wish to excel, and showing them that there is always an optimal interpretation which, though rarely achieved, must always be pursued. The novice conductor working with youth choirs can grow along with the group, seeking technical improvement step by step. It must always be clear that the main goal at any level is a superior musical interpretation. The best way to create enthusiasm and encourage a group of young choristers is to highlight the benefits that music offers, especially the satisfaction that comes with personal growth, and the sense of accomplishment after a good concert or rehearsal.

It is difficult to suggest a single technique that is equally useful to all conducting students because we are all born with different characteristics, many of them genetic, others cultural. Conductors' ambitions may vary: some are better suited to work with children and youth choirs, while others feel more comfortable working with adult ensembles. There are also those that aspire to become directors of choral-symphonic ensembles. It must be highlighted that in many cases the aspirations of directors are not always accompanied by the skills required to realize them. There are conductors who are very adept of organizing festivals and participating in national and international concert tours, and others who lack these talents.

To avoid setbacks and stumbles conductors must be conscious of their own inclinations, limitations, and attraction to specific type of work. Even very capable conductors sometimes feel driven to compete with one another, yet this leads only to disappointment and dissatisfaction. Resenting colleagues' achievements bespeaks only meanness and ignorance.

If the ideal school of choral conducting were to exist, it could only prepare students in the basic skills of the profession: elements of gesture, score analysis, music history and repertoire from different periods. What cannot be taught in any school is how to maximize the capabilities of a choir, encouraging them to give their best in both the concert and during the rehearsal process. Another aspect that cannot be taught is the indispensable intuition to discover the music beyond what is indicated in the score, because, no matter how well and precisely it is written, its essence will always be beyond the paper that contains it.

Music is expression and communication, and to decipher the content of a piece analytical tools are indispensable, but not in themselves sufficient. Intuition, sensitivity and creative power are not qualities that can be approved in any learning institution. However, one must be aware that the best intuition, sensitivity, creative power and superior talent are worth little if the conductor lacks the theory and technique that is appropriately taught in good music schools.

The well-known expression "there are no bad choirs, only poorly prepared conductors" has proven true indeed. Any conductor who is aware of the real capabilities of his ensemble and does not overextend them will usually find reason to feel satisfied with their accomplishments, and will instill in the singers the pride of giving their best.

Recommendations for the conductor:
- It is necessary to project a professional and pleasant manner in front of the choir and the audience, giving an impression of confidence, trustworthiness and respect.
- One must stand straight, but without rigidity, maintaining elegant posture without putting on airs. One can have sense of humor, but without being vulgar.
- One must acknowledge applause with a natural and kind attitude, but without false modesty. Practice a simple but thankful reverence.
- One must exude a mood that is consistent with the music being performed.
- Conducting patterns must be mastered such that the conductor is free to concentrate on the music.
- One should use discrete movements within a small range. It is more useful to use subtle movements and reserve bigger ones for special moments demanded by the music.

- Regarding the music itself, the conductor's attitude should always be to preserve and enhance what is good in each composition, trying to lend an absolute sense of truth to the understanding of the piece. The way to achieve this is by holding oneself to the highest standard, and refusing to make concessions to the easy way out and mediocrity.
- The conductor should preserve all that is good within the music, honoring past choices while committing fully to the search for a true pathway. The conductor must act in good faith to see old music with new eyes.
- One should begin with easy pieces, canons and popular songs that are attractive and joyful. At the same time, practice simple breathing, pitch and rhythm exercises.
- One must insist on progressive perfection through practical examples of how to improve.
- One should recommend that the members of the ensemble go to concerts of other choirs. They should be encouraged to celebrate social gatherings, and generally strengthen the links among the members. New singers must be inculcated into a culture that values artistic projects.
- One must emphasize discipline in the group to fight against lack of responsibility and absenteeism. One must emphasize total engagement in the choral rehearsal in order to achieve personal musical progress.
- One should advocate for the choral program with the administrators of the institution, explaining the advantages of choral music and soliciting their approval and support. If the authorities feel well represented by the choir it can be a symbol of institutional pride and satisfaction.

- One should try to transform choral activity into a central part of the life of the organization which the ensemble represents.
- On occasion the conductor will have the opportunity to collaborate with instrumentalists in chamber or choral-symphonic works. Do not miss out on these opportunities, as both choir and conductor benefit greatly. This is why the acquisition of knowledge in orchestral conducting is necessary in the education of choral conductors, even if this is not their central role. This will allow the conductor to successfully tackle works of varying complexities including choral-orchestral works.

The same recommendation is likewise valid for orchestral conductors who are sometimes lacking in choral background and unable to achieve the best possible results in performances involving singers.

Selecting Repertoire

When talking about repertoire the following questions are vital: Does the piece being considered have expressive possibilities? Is it a viable project for the choir, or does it serve primarily to satisfy the conductor's ego or self-image of the choir? Does it challenge the choir with technical and artistic requirements that are beyond their capabilities? Does it offer sufficient interest, or is it chosen just to "have a good time" without great musical expectations?

When dealing with a group it is nearly impossible to satisfy everyone's diverse tastes. One model is the professional ensemble where procedures, schedules, repertoire, honoraria, etc. are clearly defined, and in which there is little opportunity for members to participate in artistic decisions. This is not the ideal, nor the most common model, for frequently in this case not even the conductor has significant input into the selection of repertoire, and often must prepare a determined piece on a predetermined timeline.

For any competent director with good intentions to prepare the choir with musicality and detail it is advisable to make a prior assessment, no matter how approximate, of the real capabilities of the ensemble so that adequate rehearsal time can be dedicated to the work in question, ensuring a good outcome.

When tackling new repertoire it is necessary to energize the entire choral team from the very first rehearsal, encouraging the group to work with enthusiasm and dedication. During the rehearsal process the conductor should be attentive to progress with more difficult pieces, which will help develop expand the capabilities of the choir. If at concert time they are not yet at an appropriate level for public performance, the director must cut these works from the program and wait for another chance to take them up again. These opportunities will surely present themselves in the right moment.

It is wise not to set unreachable goals, which, in the end, will create unnecessary frustration. Similarly, one should not present the choir in choral competitions with very difficult repertoire when the group is not ready for it as this will lead to failure, and inevitably to declining motivation and energy. There are beautiful and simple choral compositions, both *a cappella* and accompanied by instruments, which can be sung by choirs with limited musicianship. The conductor must know how to choose repertoire that corresponds with the capabilities of the group, and how to avoid succumbing to external pressures and suggestions of compositions that are inappropriate for the ensemble.

Choral Repertoire

Historical Background

Music is one of our most refined cultural practices. It is very probable that its origin is as old as humanity itself, and that its initial utterance must have been more closely related to an unarticulated shout or a percussive noise than to those elements that nowadays are part of its phonetics, syntax and semantics. It is remarkable that humans have created such a complex and beautiful language using such primitive elements.

Throughout the centuries musical styles have adapted to the social realities of their time and place. From the varied and complex modal system inherited from ancient cultures, the Ionian and Aeolian modes emerged. These were then transformed into pur modern major and minor scales, respectively. Equal temperament, which set the distance between contiguous notes at equal half-step intervals, allowed greater flexibility in the use of modulation which was formerly restricted to closely-related keys. Between the 18th and the 19th centuries, music was based largely on the principles of common practice tonality. From a historical point of view, the arrival of the 20th century brought stark changes that would accelerate technical progress but also result in greater human tensions, inequality, and insecurity of states and people. Society moved from a carefree, light-hearted *belle époque* of the Victorian era to the brutal tension of the First World War.

As sensitive barometers of society, artists could not be unaffected by these events. After the light-filled and timeless aesthetics of Impressionism came the anguish and turbulence of Expressionism. Writers, painters and musicians expressed the growing social malaise in works charged with fear for a society that had lost its way. In music, the Second Viennese School, represented by composer Arnold Schönberg[32] and his most relevant disciples (Berg, Webern, etc.), embodied these tendencies. With the decay of the tonal system the door to 12-tone and serialist composition was open, and in post-war Europe bitonal, atonal, or even polytonal music held sway.

The 20th century has been a period of constant conflicts, battles and political disturbances in which the world became very "noisy." Music was not unaffected by the reality of its surroundings, and "noise" entered musical language. To the simple *alla turca* percussion of the 18th century a multitude of instruments were added, both pitched and unpitched, which suited this new sound concept.

A significant amount of choral music has been composed in the 20th century representing many diverse genres: opera, oratorio, sacred and secular cantata, choral symphonies, *a cappella* and accompanied pieces, music for choirs and soloists, etc. Time will tell which of these tendencies continue the great musical tradition of the West and its natural evolution and which are fleeting fashions or musical dead ends.

The Conductor and Contemporary Music

The conductor must be aware that the tonal/modal system is a varied and rich source for what the composer wants to communicate. In the contemporary emergence

---

[32] Arnold Schönberg (1874-1951). Creator of dodecaphonism, a technique of serial composition later enriched by his disciples.

of multiple concurrent musical styles tonality has not disappeared; on the contrary, it has been enriched. The conductor of contemporary music is called upon to shape diverse combinations of styles and influences, and therefore must understand and know how to choose from the immense assortment of forms and acoustic possibilities inherited from many centuries of musical evolution.

When listeners' ears are accustomed to conventional tonal music, many compositions written in completely contemporary styles can engender boredom, disgust or rejection. The audience must never be underestimated; it is for them that one writes and performs. Even composers of electronic music whose compositions were largely dependent on synthesized sounds nonetheless felt compelled to write works that mixed pre-recorded tape with live musicians in order to attract an audience towards a music that was, until that moment, unlikely to be played in a concert hall in front of an audience.

Aleatoric music has also permeated choral repertoire. Throughout music history a certain freedom was inherent in the great tradition of improvisation, but it was well into the 20th century before free aleatoric composition took hold. Music that is completely aleatoric is not very popular nowadays as it is considered financially unfeasible for most concert programs. However, choral works that introduce some "controlled" aleatoric elements are rather common.

When performing aleatoric music, the conductor should explain the background and meaning of the compositional style to the choir. After studying the piece and understanding its notation, which will usually be new and frequently created by the composer, choir and conductor must together seek new expressive means for its interpretation.

As the great mirror of history, art reflects the fragmentation, alienation and vertigo of modern life. Some contemporary music might not be attractive because it appears to be a *collage* of disparate styles, but its appeal lies in how it reflects our way of life and the reality of our scattered society. Generally, given the difficulty of some contemporary musical styles, it is better for pieces of experimental nature to be performed by professional ensembles.

Certainly conductors must be familiar with their time and the vanguard tendencies of the period. This does not mean, however, that they are obligated to interpret music that may not be the most appropriate for their ensembles. They must first and foremost engender interest and enthusiasm in their groups towards choral music. Yet the door should be left open for new musical compositions of high artistic value if and when they meet the artistic criteria of the ensemble. Creative exploration of unusual repertoire will give composers and directors the opportunity to explore novel effects, broadening their expressive palette.

This array of new alternatives also provides an opportunity to incorporate different performance aspects, which could include body movement, eurhythmics, varied staging, and interpretative choreography. Movement has also been demonstrated to be very effective in children's, youth and adult choirs. Liberated from the rigidity of traditional choirs, choristers are often inspired to participate with enthusiasm in this type of music. Finally, it is important to highlight the value of selecting repertoire of composers from different periods, styles and levels, if appropriate to the artistic mission of the ensemble.

Choir/Conductor Relationship

An environment of healthy camaraderie, that is to say sincere trust and mutual loyalty, is an essential foundation for the choir-conductor relationship. Warm and open communication with the entire group will facilitate good music-making. Perhaps one of the greatest challenges for a conductor is to know how much can be demanded from the choristers, and how to convince them to commit themselves fully to the ensemble.

In a choir, every member usually has his or her particular ideas regarding what the goals of the group should be. The reasons singers choose to join a choir can also be quite personal. Some are there because they want to raise their level of vocal technique and musicianship. Others join because of their love for music, or to seek a social outlet that engenders friendships based on memorable moments shared with their peers.

Although every one of the members may want to achieve a good result in each concert, it is not always easy to motivate them to give their best effort to do so. The director must find the best method for consistent artistic improvement, keeping in mind the heterogeneous nature of the group. This requires sensitivity in dealing with human relationships and familiarity with each choir member, which will allow the conductor to correctly evaluate their strengths and weaknesses.

The general principle is to begin a rehearsal or performance in the most positive state of mind. The conductor who offers an affectionate smile to the group before starting an activity is already guaranteed a certain level of success in his or her engagement as a leader. Nonetheless, small human conflicts, which are not always avoidable, can negatively affect the performance of a choir. When issues present themselves they must be solved quickly, so that they do not create tension or discomfort. Often these problems can be resolved with a sincere and calm conversation. If the situation persists, the conductor should relocate the person with the issue to a place where there is less visual contact, making his or her presence less uncomfortable and negative until the issue has been resolved. During a rehearsal, unpleasant interactions between the conductor and a choir member may result in a loss of concentration and an aesthetically or technically unsatisfactory result for the choir.

Sometimes these situations between members of the choir or between the conductor and singers can unfortunately last long periods of time. It is important to avoid conflicts as much as possible, and resolve them quickly when they do arise. Usually the passage of time heals these problems, but when the pressures become chronic, it can be better for the conductor to ask these members to leave the choir. Small problems must be resolved with all possible expediency such that they do not become big problems that will be reflected in the artistic quality of the group.

It sometimes happens that the person who generates tension in the ensemble also has the greatest vocal gift. One might think that it would be unfortunate to lose such talent, but experience has demonstrated again and again that it is better to lose the good voice, which could be substituted later on, than to negatively affect the group because of the presence of a disturbing member. With the removal of the "problem-member," the improvement of the environment will favor a more positive attitude in both the conductor and choristers, which in turn will encourage all the singers to give their best effort.

Conflicts can be dealt with relatively easily in situations where professional ensembles exist, where the conductor has the ability to modify the roster, relocating or substituting as he or she chooses. If a chorister generates conflicts, he or she is replaced with another of similar artistic level. This is not the case in when the majority of the choirs are amateur, where there is difficulty finding good singers, or where there is bad energy among the choristers, or between the singers and the conductor.

The conductor-chorister relationship will be most productive when there is mutual friendship and trust, and good communication. In this environment of respect, it will be possible for ideas, suggestions, and innovations to flow freely without undermining the authority of the conductor.

A conductor who is able to earn the trust and recognition of fellow artists will always achieve better artistic results. Professional training, acquired in conservatories and institutions of higher education, conducting workshops and graduate programs, does not guarantee the full gamut of capabilities required to become an effective conductor. It is not enough to be a well-trained and talented musician in order to become a successful leader of a choir. One must also be able to motivate and engage others.

With every public performance there is pressure that can lead to anxiety for the conductor. Overcoming this fear, though difficult, is essential. Above and beyond the artistic demands, the conductor's responsibilities around performance time often include many small but vital procedural decisions, and excessive anxiety can spread uneasiness to the whole ensemble, with negative consequences for the aesthetic and artistic results of the event.

A good director must know how to confront fear, transforming it into assertive and productive work. Thus, as a rule, every conductor must set a time aside for serene insight and self-reflection, evaluating feelings and exploring the quality of connections with the choir and with each chorister in particular. Conductors should use this meditation to cultivate an attitude that is consistent with the artistic results they seek.

Institutional Obligations

Although conductors are specialists in music with artistic duties, their administrative responsibilities are equally important. These often include reporting to the institution that sponsors the choir they conduct. Consequently, the conductor must maintain an optimal communication with the board, or private or public institution, allowing a fluent and positive relationship for the better functioning of the choir as an entity.

The conductor must work to maintain a flexible and reasonable attitude towards the people or entities on which the existence of the choir depends. Sometimes this will involve accepting recommendations made in good faith, but lacking in musical knowledge or aesthetic and artistic sensitivity. The conductor must not assume an intransigent attitude that risks the stability of the team, but rather must try to find ways of maintaining communication, modifying suggestions or finding ways to reject them without creating bitterness. Cordiality and the constant pursuit of harmonious relations with sponsoring institutions are fundamental skills that will help the conductor avoid uncomfortable situations and disappointments that negatively impact the stability of the ensemble.

Chapter 4
The Choir

The Quality of the Group

*"This little world of choirs is a mirror
of the whole human race."*

César Ferreyra

The quality of a choral group is dependent on multiple factors, all of which, directly or indirectly, are affected by the conductor of the ensemble. Because choirs are complex entities defined by both human and purely musical elements, to define a "good choir" is quite difficult. Pinpointing exactly the qualities that define it is a subjective process not unlike that of quantifying the aesthetic qualities of a piece of music. As more subjective observations concur it can be said that we begin to approach greater objectivity. We offer here some observations concerning quality in the hope of inspiring conductors to achieve the highest possible levels of choral singing with their ensembles.

A Good Choir

How can a choir be judged as good or bad? What would be the "ideal choir?" What parameters would be used to label a musical organization as "excellent," or "the best choral group?" Is any such judgment, by its very nature, fleeting or temporary? Do the judges who confer these labels act in a spirit of fairness and consistency, letting themselves be guided by a consistent set of aesthetic principles?

In order to create a choir of high quality one must have good choristers, which is by no means a small consideration. One has to take into account that in the majority of cases a good chorister is educated over time, singing and developing other human virtues such as community, tolerance, discipline, etc. The good chorister is therefore "not born, but made" as a result of many hours and days of preparation and experience. Perhaps what is most fundamental is the desire and vocation to sing in a group, love of music, commitment, enthusiasm and dedication to the ensemble. In addition to these qualities singers must also cultivate their vocal gifts and develop their music reading skills.

A very common mistake is to make a snap judgment in deciding whether or not a person is capable of singing in a choir. To judge an aspirant and "label" him or her for life on the basis of a brief audition can be both a very negative experience for the singer, and also an inaccurate measure of the singer's capabilities. Snap judgments of this kind are doubly harmful when applied to choosing younger choristers, whose skills are still developing and changing rapidly. The ideal method of achieving good results in the recruitment of choristers is a procedure of evaluation over a longer period of time in which both singer and conductor can get a fuller sense of what they offer to each other, and to the group.

In his book *Cuentos Corales (Choral Tales)* Maestro César Ferreyra writes:

"In my life I have given thousands of auditions to aspiring choristers. I regret every one of them, even when the results were apparently accurate. The missing factor is the duration of the evaluation. It is necessary to take time to get to know the candidate, for him or her to get to know their fellow choristers and director, to understand their assets and defects, and to integrate them into this little world of choirs that is a mirror of the entire human race. It can take days, weeks or even months for the singer to fully enter with body, soul, heart and mind into these new surroundings. Taking this time offers true assurance of the suitability of the candidate far superior to the pretentious calculations designed to get to know a person and an artist in five minutes."

It is worth remembering that when we talk about good choirs, we are referring to all kinds of ensembles, whether made up of amateurs, non-professional musicians or professional choristers, and whether they are in mixed choirs, treble choirs, children's choirs, etc.

Sadly, in some cultures or social settings little importance is given to the study of singing. This is especially the case with children, who are led to believe that whereas reading, writing, arithmetic and sports are compulsory, learning music and choral singing are fun, but inessential experiences. In only a few countries around the world is music an important subject in the school curriculum.

Among children's choirs one possible structure is the school choir, in which singers are organized by grade level rather than musical talent. These choirs are usually created to fulfill an institutional need and often do not address music will mean in the future life of these young singers. We cannot expect great artistic results from choirs that are organized along this model, which is foreign to both the art and to the individual education of the child. Yet who can deny that such a choir could become an "ideal chorus" to one particular energetic conductor and the young members of the ensemble? Children may value their group highly, especially if they are under the direction of a caring and motivating teacher who is dedicated to their emotional and aesthetic growth, and who encourages them to love the choir and to feel joy in participating in rehearsals and concerts. Their families could also come to believe that theirs is the "ideal choir," and rightly so if their children value and benefit from their experience.

Other children's groups belong to music schools or institutions, whose interests differ from traditional school choirs. Here, there is greater selectivity based on vocal quality and musical talent. Better compensation for conductors leads to greater commitment and more challenging repertoire.

Regardless of any public success, from a social and educational point of view, both lesser-trained choirs and those trained to compete internationally have the same reason to exist, and thus should feel the same enjoyment, satisfaction, and pride. To disdain any of their efforts would be neither fair nor advisable. We should always keep in mind that there exists a huge range of choirs, from the apparently most insignificant choir to the most internationally acclaimed ensembles.

We can say that "the ideal" children's choir is the one that is made up of children who have the good fortune and privilege of making music, and appreciate the joy of singing. This is equally valid for adult choral ensembles, be they treble, mixed, chamber, church, secular or professional choirs. By definition, the choir is always good in that it serves to allow a group of human beings to come together to communicate through music, our most sublime form of expression.

Given the wide variety of structures and experiences, it is challenging to establish music education programs that impart sufficient knowledge and training to ensure that young singers continue to participate in choirs and develop their musical abilities. Moreover, there are many negative societal influences that expose young people to unhealthy lifestyles, and devalue any activity that develops a greater spiritual practice through choral music.

It is a pity to witness the ever-decreasing participation of children and youth in choral music. Years of experience working with children's choirs have shown that when they are exposed to excellent music under inspiring conductors, children participate with great enthusiasm in choral singing. The failure to take part in choral activities is due, in large part, to the lack of support from parents for an educational activity that they do not understand. It is not unusual to hear adults refer to artistic activity and training as irrelevant for facing the challenges of modern society. In fact nothing could be further from the truth.

This complex situation challenges choral directors, who must fight against deeply rooted negative societal attitudes towards participation in music. It is worth repeating the belief that any human being from any society (perhaps with the exception of those with physical issues that impede vocal control) can, given time, patience and dedication, sing in tune well enough to participate in a choir.

Professional choirs, despite their variety of mission and repertoire, are defined by the common denominator that their members are paid to sing. These choirs work at different levels and in varying structures, most of them formed by people with extensive choral experience, cultivated voices and good musicianship. Because of their professional standards it would be natural to presume that these ensembles are better equipped for presenting more difficult repertoire and that it is easy for them to present a greater variety of programs than amateur choirs. One might also imagine that the professional nature of the ensemble would ensure that the members are highly motivated to prepare, rehearse and present concerts. However, it is not unusual to find a greater level of dedication and enjoyment in amateur choirs, where choristers sing for the pleasure of music making, for the joy of belonging to a beloved ensemble, and for the sense of community.

In many cases, choral conductors therefore prefer working with choirs that are not professional, but nonetheless of a good musical level. The groups can often dedicate longer periods of time to learning repertoire, and are therefore able to explore music at a deeper level, yielding greater satisfaction for the conductor, choristers and audience. The ideal situation might then be a choir that has both the voices and knowledge of professional choristers and the enthusiasm and devotion common among amateur choristers. When these ensembles are formed we are in the presence of music in all its splendor and greatness.

Cantoría Juvenil de la Schola Cantorum de Venezuela, The World of Children's Voices Festival, Vancouver, Canada, 2002. Conductor: Cristian Grases

Schola Cantorum de Venezuela, Auditory Alfredo Kraus, Las Palmas de Gran Canarias, España, 2009.
Pasión según San Marcos by Osvaldo Golijov.

Schola Juvenil de Venezuela, Caracas, Venezuela, 2007

Great Organ, Inaugural Concert. Main Hall, Centro de Acción Social por la Música, Caracas, Venezuela, 2008. Conductor: María Guinand

Chapter 5

Essential Elements of Music

Rhythm

*"A small sound impulse is closer to the point
of return or rest than a large one."*

Sergiu Celibidache

Rhythm is a periodic succession of pulses, joined in combinations of sounds and rests. The defining characteristic of musical flow is the relationship between its impulse and resolution (*arsis* and *thesis*). Because a completely detailed and precise system to represent musical concepts does not exist, all music notation is necessarily an approximation, based on a system organized principally around rhythmic phenomena.

When a regular series of undifferentiated pulses reaches our senses we perceive rhythm. Our consciousness then organizes these perceptions into the larger relationships that characterize musical structure, introducing accents that define the otherwise undistinguished aural phenomena. Our natural tendency is to take an undifferentiated series of rhythmic impulses (♩♩♩♩♩♩ etc.), and organize it into rhythmic units in either binary (♩♩) or ternary meter (♩♩♩).

Heaviness and Laxity

Through the process of discernment mentioned above, single undifferentiated notes become part of a hierarchy based on either dynamics or intensity. Some notes take on weight, while others are light and deferent.

No note can be strong without one or two weak neighbors, and similarly no note can be lax unless it is associated with another that is strong. The association of these qualities, heaviness and laxity, is the primary foundation of every musical perception, and is the basis for complex musical thought.

Tempo

In all musical discourse there is a tempo (or speed), which is determined not only by the piece itself, but also other factors such as venue, acoustics of the performing space, quality of the ensemble, etc. Finding an optimal tempo is imperative for a good performance; thus, the conductor must be attentive to the many subtle elements that can vary from moment to moment.

Articulation

Articulation, often defined in terms of *legato*, *marcato*, etc. can also refer to the division of each pulse into its constituent elements. Understood in this sense articulation can be fast (many small notes) or slow (few subdivisions of the pulse) within any given tempo.

Taking that definition of articulation as a starting point we realize that without it there could be no music, for music requires the relationship between the original impulse and its resolution. One note alone or a single chord cannot be defined as music because it lacks the fragmentation and sequence produced by articulation, be it a Bach chorale, a simple Gregorian melody, the most involved polyphonic composition, or a choral-symphonic masterwork of great complexity.

One of the essential elements of musical artistry is being able to organize and interpret the innumerable articulations in their most appropriate formulas and variations.

When the tempo (and the articulation of each pulse) is too fast or slow, music can lose expressiveness and quality. Some interpreters use extremely fast tempos in order to disguise a lack of interpretative gifts. When tempo is too slow coherence in the musical discourse suffers.

‖‖‖‖‖‖‖‖‖‖	Articulation is too fast
| | | | | | |	Articulation is ideal
| | | |	Articulation is too slow

Pulse

As the basic unit of rhythm, pulse is the reference point with which the conductor's gesture indicates the music. The pulse can be subdivided, elongated, or contracted without altering in any way its basic function.

Relationship between Pulse and Articulation

Conducting gestures are meant to beat or mark the pulse to reflect the organic relationship between the body and music. Each level of perception related to pulse and tempo can be reflected in the gesture.

When the tempo is faster, figures are less differentiated. When the tempo is slower, there is more differentiation within each figure or pulse. This means that the slower the articulation, the greater the capacity to distinguish and appreciate smaller detail.

Example of the pulse-articulation relationship

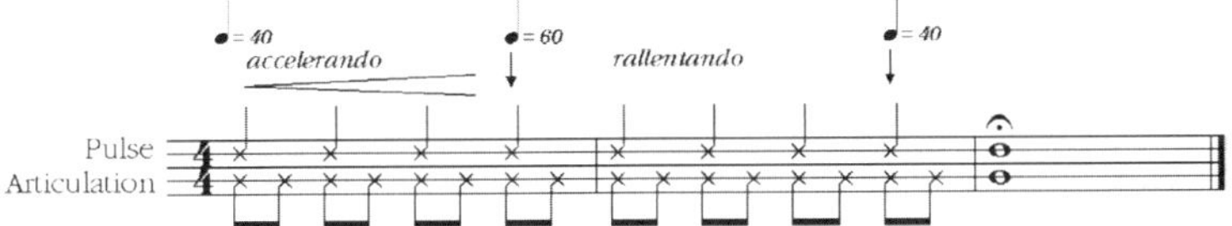

Establishing the pulse

It is important to be clear when discussing the meaning of pulse. Tempo is necessarily elastic, as there must be a certain flexibility to accommodate the natural and indispensable variations inherent in every interpretation.

In the case of mixed meter the conductor's initial concern must be finding a common unit between the preparatory gesture (upbeat) and the first beat of the music. The director must search for the most convenient unit of pulse to organize and clarify changes in meter or tempo. Every change of tempo must be accomplished using the unit of pulse of the new articulation and anticipating the new tempo.

When negotiating these changes of tempo or meter it is vital to find a unit of pulse that connects the sections in an organic way. Sometimes the music itself requires sudden changes, but when not, finding a natural and unobtrusive way to negotiate these changes smoothly is preferred. Consider the following exercises excerpted from the first and third movements of Igor Stravinsky's *Symphony of Psalms.*

Rios Reyna Hall, Teresa Carreño Theater. Gustav Mahler's Symphony No. 8, Caracas, Venezuela, 1988. Conductor: Teo Alcántara

Symphony of Psalms

Igor Stravinsky (1822-1971)

Rhythmic outline for large score memorization,
and practicing changes in tempo, accents etc.

First Movement

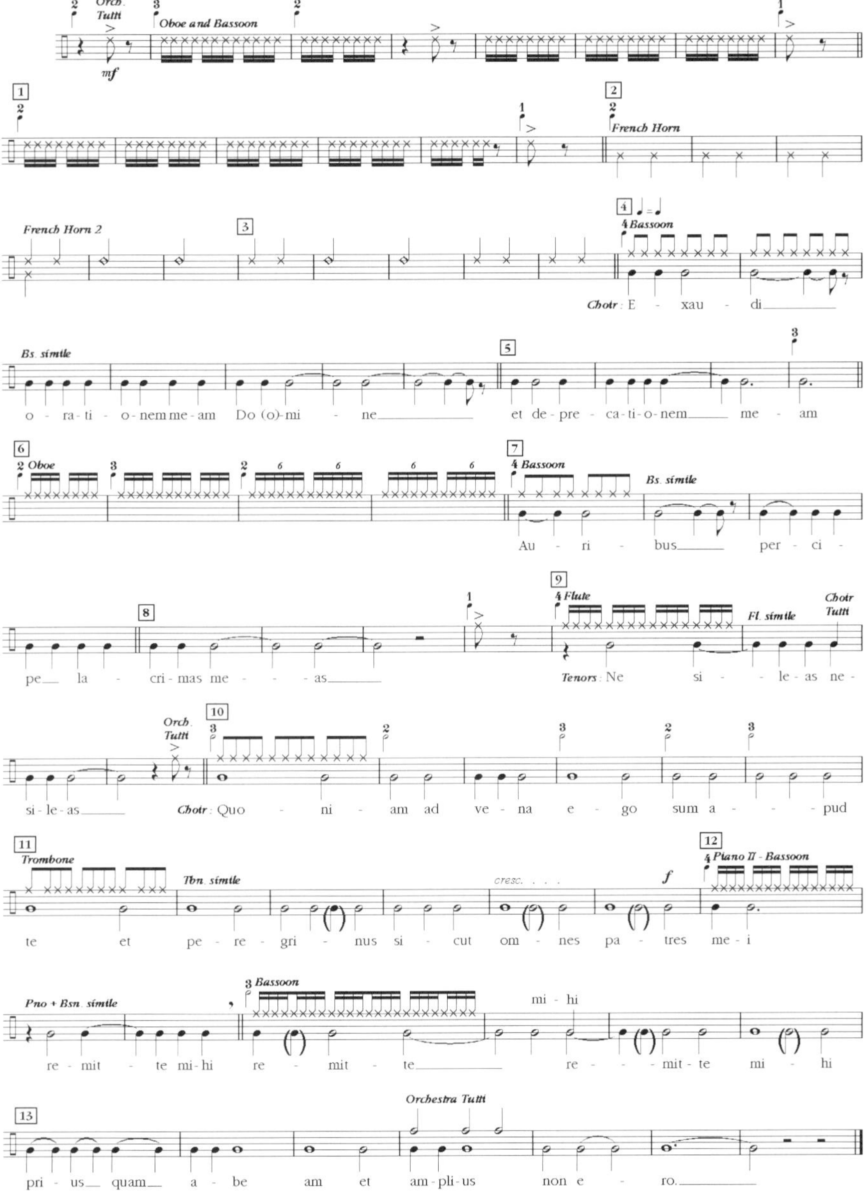

Third Movement

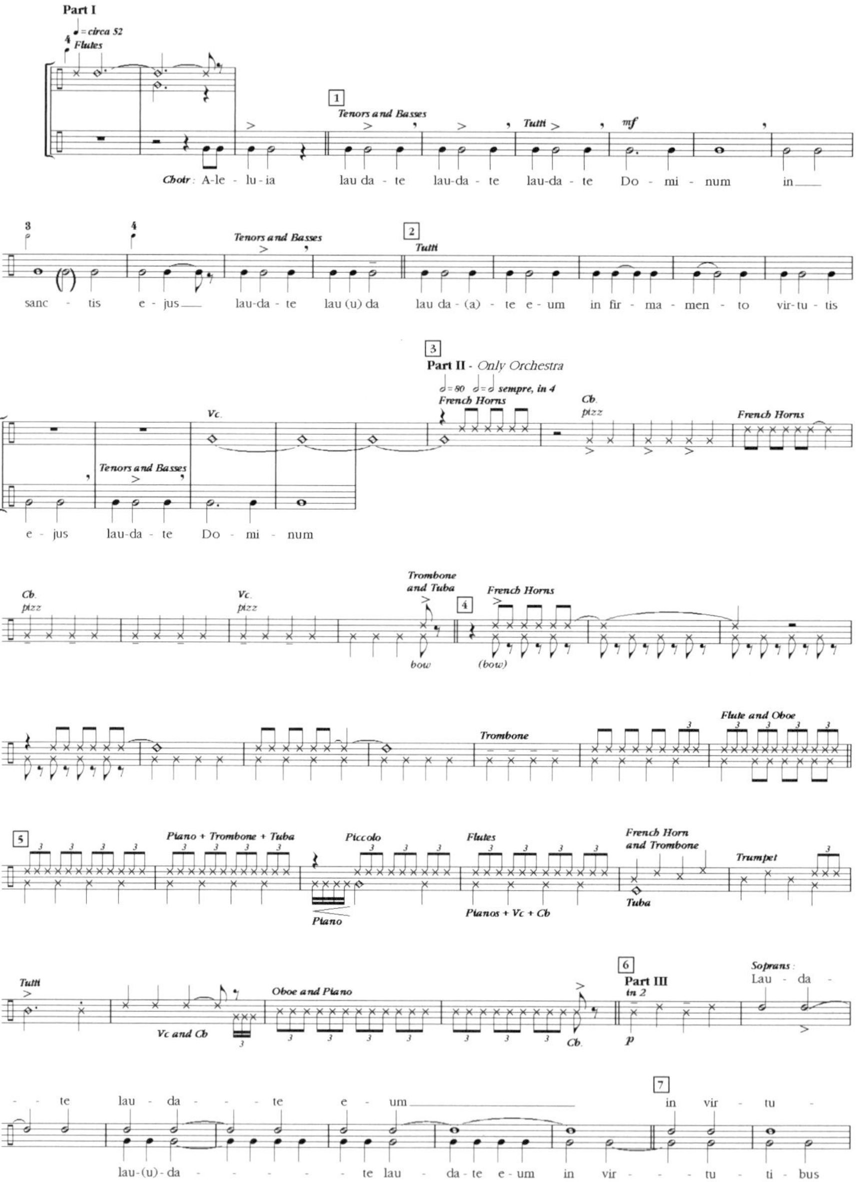

ti - bus e - jus
e - jus
Altos and Tenors
8
lau da-te Do-mi num in vir - tu-ti bus e - jus lau da te
Do-mi num in sanc - tis e - jus
Basses: lau - da - - te e - um se -
9
2
3
cun - dum mul - ti - tu - si - nem mag...etc
e - um se -
10
Lau - da - te
3
2
Soprans: lau - da - te e - um in so - (ho) - no tu - (hu) -
- - cun - dum mul - ti - tu - di - nem mag - ni -
11
- - bæ lau - da - te e - (he) - um
tu - di - nem e - um
Bassoon
Part IV
Lento ♩= 48
12
Tutti: A-le -
lu - ia lau - da - te Do-mi-num lau - da - te e - um
♩= 80 in 4
sfp
3
French Horn
Trombone
French Horn 1
13
Trombone
4
in 3
3
Choir: lau da - te Do-mi-num
Piano
Bassoon
and Vc.
14
French Horn
sfz
Choir: lau da - te Do-mi num
15
16
Trombone
Tbn + Vc + Cb
Choir: lau da te Do-mi num
Tbn + Vc + Cb
Flutes
3
3
3
3
3
3
3
3
3
3
3
17
Trombone and Tuba
Choir: Lau da-te Do-mi num
lau-da-te e-um

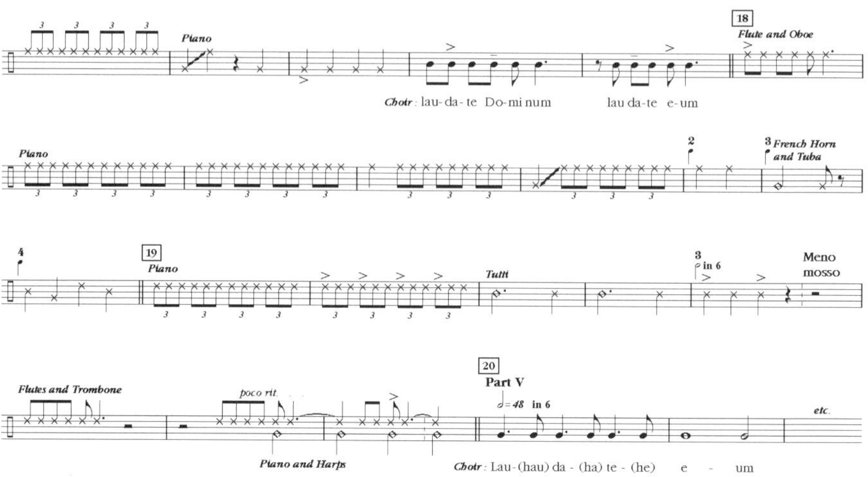

Pulse and gesture

Generally, the speed of the gesture is inversely proportionate to the number of articulations between one ictus and the next. In other words, more rhythmic activity yields fewer inflection points or visible subdivisions of the ictus between pulses. With less rhythmic activity the quantity of inflections in the gesture can be greater.

The proportion between pulse and articulation can be direct or inverse.

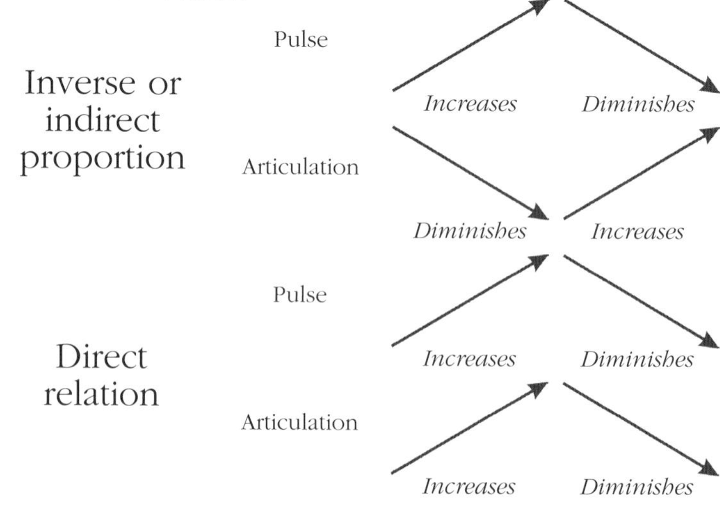

Example of the relation between pulse and gesture

Pulse = articulation in the gesture

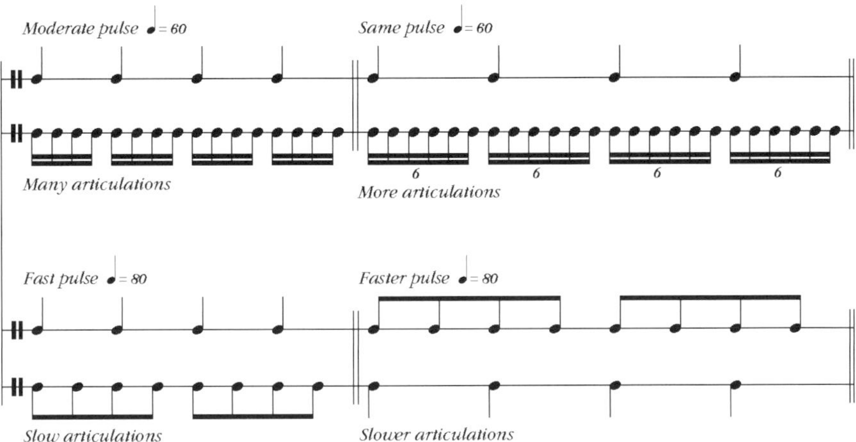

Example of the relation between pulse and gesture
From "Salmo 150" by Ernani Aguiar (1950-)

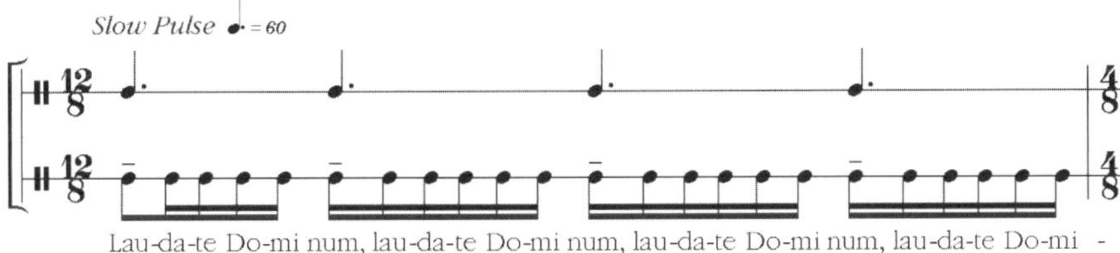

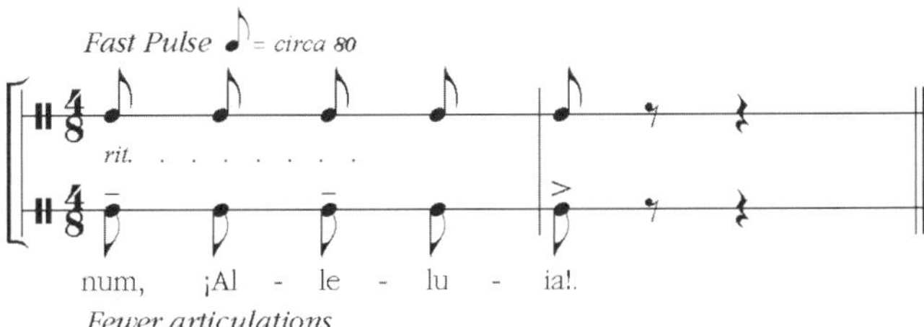

Example of a same pulse
with different articulations

From "El Santiguao" by Federico Ruiz (1948-).

Accent

Generally speaking, grammatical and musical accents should be directly related. Exceptions to this occur due to the figures that precede or follow these accents or because of gestural requirements before or after rhythmic accents.

Musical accent need not necessarily coincide with the downbeat. To prepare an accent from a gestural perspective, the space or distance that the arm usually travels within the already established pulse must be increased. After the gesture is extended, the speed must be accelerated in order to avoid being late to the next ictus.

Even when the downbeat does not coincide with the musical accent, the listener will still perceive the hierarchy of the barline if the measure is correctly written. This is true despite the fact that other notes within that measure may be accented.

The following exercises are useful to practice many types of accents in varying places in the conducting pattern. Note: if these exercises are practiced at slower speeds, the patterns must be modified.

Exercise 1. Different Types of Accents

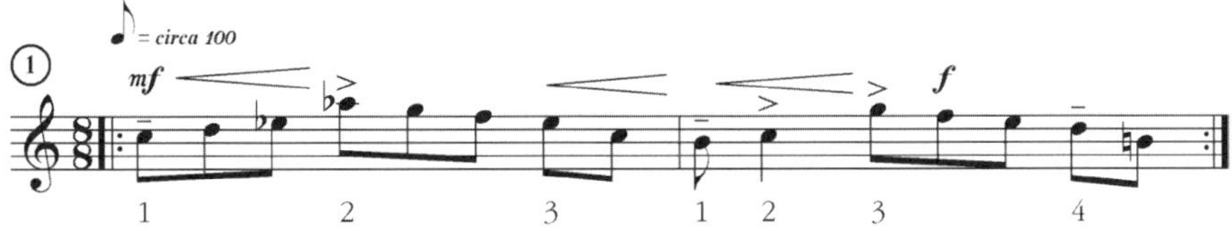

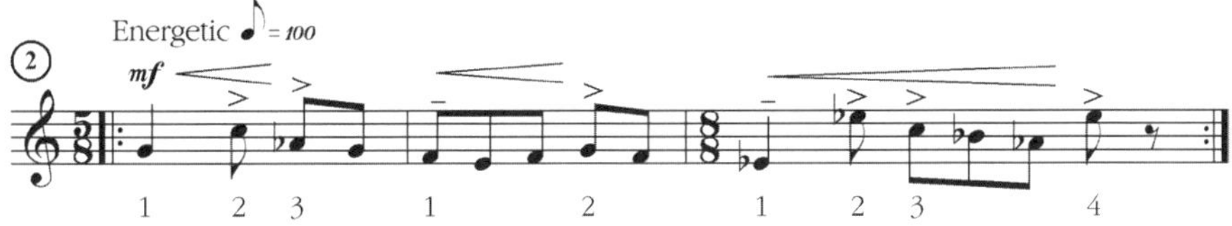

Exercise 2. Different Types of Accents

Begin by studying each exercise separately, then combine them sequentially.

Any simple melody has a musical flow with natural rhythmic highpoints, which can sometimes be modified for harmonic reasons. The following exercises can be used to practice recognition of various patterns within a measure.

Exercise 3. Beating irregular meters

Based on G. Hahn's (1908-2001) composition "Rondo Laponico" (Sweden, 1971)

Shaping, Phrasing and Interpretation

One of the conductor's tasks is to shape the music according to its points of magnetic attraction, the areas of greater or lesser strength or tension inherent in the musical flow. When melodic or harmonic progressions are tied to a poetic text, these magnetic poles are easier to recognize and interpret because they are associated with the poetic structure.

Sometimes the melodic line does not correspond with the text setting. In these cases, it is almost always wisest to give priority to the text, as music should always be at the service of poetry. Occasionally there are exceptions to this that require that the music take priority over the text. Such situations generally arise due to an error on the part of the composer, for it is poetry that serves as the initial impulse that generates a composition, and should therefore be the determinative element in the composition.

All musical discourse has a natural flow that defines its character, be it a single, homogeneous affect or a heterogeneous mosaic. Because this character is largely dependent on the speed of articulations the conductor must take into account the optimal way to handle them in order to achieve better expressive coherence.

Musical phrasing over the course of a piece results in a sum that is greater than its parts. It is a synergetic phenomenon, that is to say, one in which each successive phrase reacts to, expands on, and illuminates the last. With this in mind we realize that regardless of the lack of dynamic indications antique polyphony can be interpreted with a wide range of dynamics, *crescendo, diminuendo, accelerando, rallentando* or changes of tempo. In the 16th century these concepts were already understood by composers such as Monteverdi, Frescobaldi and Praetorius, whose music can be most logically shaped according to the natural dynamics and other details suggested by the musical flow.

Every interpretation is in some way incomplete in that it highlights and reveals certain elements while leaving others in shadow. It must ultimately bear the personal stamp of the conductor, who infuses it with creativity and spirituality based on a deep and mature study of the score. This is the only way in which magical and unrepeatable musical moments can be fully appreciated.

Vittorio Gassman said: "When an actor, while interpreting a rather intense scene, reaches a high level of intensity, he must, in order to achieve subsequent effects, lower the tone in order to begin to build again." This same rule can be applied to the concept of musical interpretation proposed above.

These concepts of interpretation are widely held by many musicians, and are as simple as they are profound and clear. We add this thought from the 20th century Catalonian musician, Pau Casals:

"There are no stereotypical styles through which music from one period or another should be interpreted. Every work, regardless of the composer or period, and without any preconceived ideas, must be submitted to a profound and detailed study with the intention of extracting the complete message of the composer. Once you become identified with it, you recreate it, giving it a life of its own. This is the only way an artist can deliver a complete version of the piece. We should not use, when interpreting early music, a reduced technique under the pretext of limitations of the period from which the score dates. On the contrary, we must use all the technical resources in our reach, including the most modern ones, in order to give the greatest possible prominence to its sonorous beauty. The most important thing is that the composition awaken pure emotion and profoundly penetrate the soul of the audience."

Three examples of dynamics, phrasing and interpretation follow, based on compositions by Johann Sebastian Bach, Francisco Guerrero and Tomás Luis de Victoria.

Example of phrasing
and interpretation of a score

Melody taken from the Chorale of the Cantata No. 147
by Johann Sebastian Bach (1685-1750)

Example of phrasing
and interpretation of a score
Melody taken from the song "Niño Dios" by Francisco Guerrero (1527?-1599)

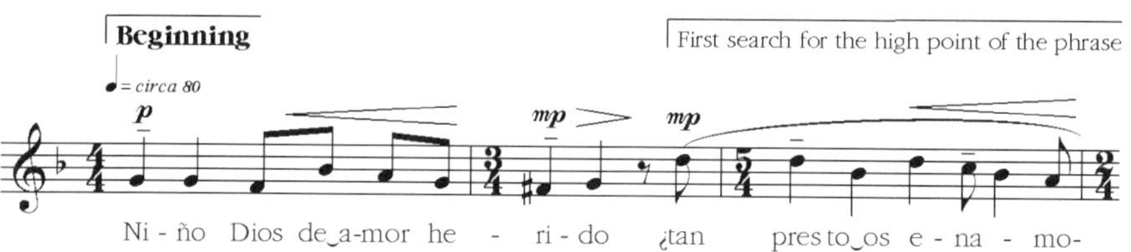

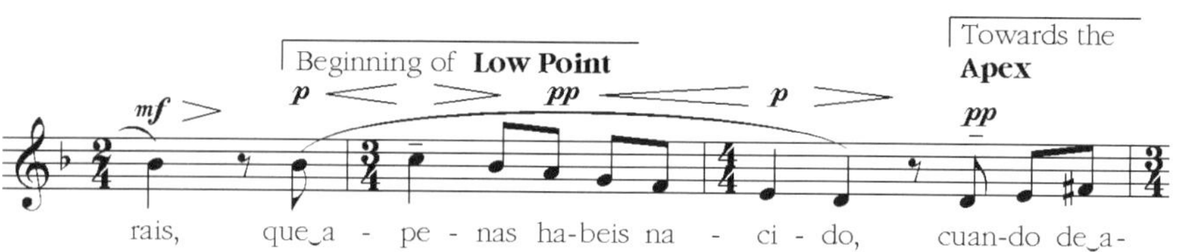

Example of phrasing
and interpretation of a score
Section of "O magnum mysterium" by Tomás Luis de Victoria (c. 1548-1611)

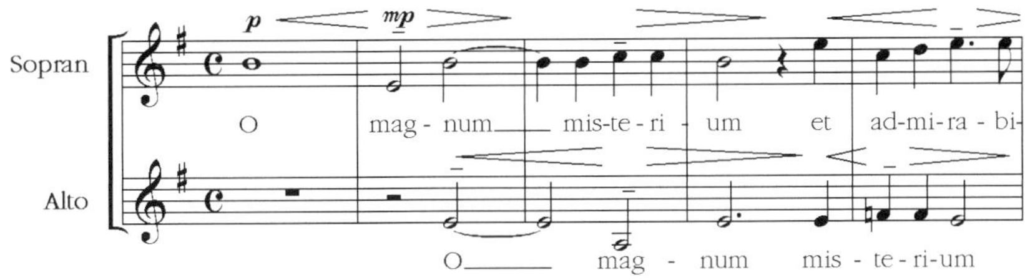

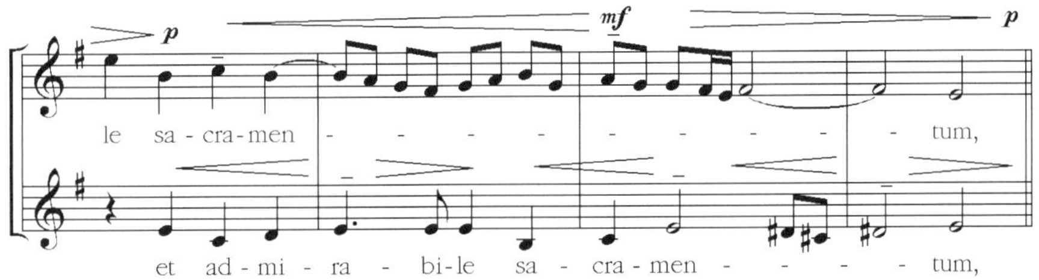

In a contrapuntal piece such as this, the accents and dynamics must happen independently in each voice. Thus the interpretation must be conceived horizontally, as its low and climactic points do not coincide vertically, except in a select few moments.

Eurhythmics

From the Greek *Eu* = good, and *ritmus* = rhythm. It is very important to feel music holistically, involving one's entire body. Rhythmic exercises are vital, and can include clapping or stomping simultaneously combined with singing. Early exposure to this kind of corporal expression contributes to the development of sensitivity in musical interpretation.

If done in the early stages of a child's musical education, this practice will help the future conductor or chorister develop a sense of rhythm and greater independence. It has been demonstrated that children who practice this type of exercise during early stages of development are less inhibited as adults and have greater concentration:

1) Polyrhythm: the simultaneous occurrence of two or more distinct rhythmic patterns.

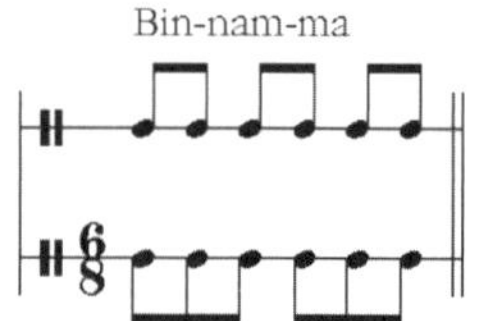

2) Polymeter: the simultaneous combination of two or more different meters.

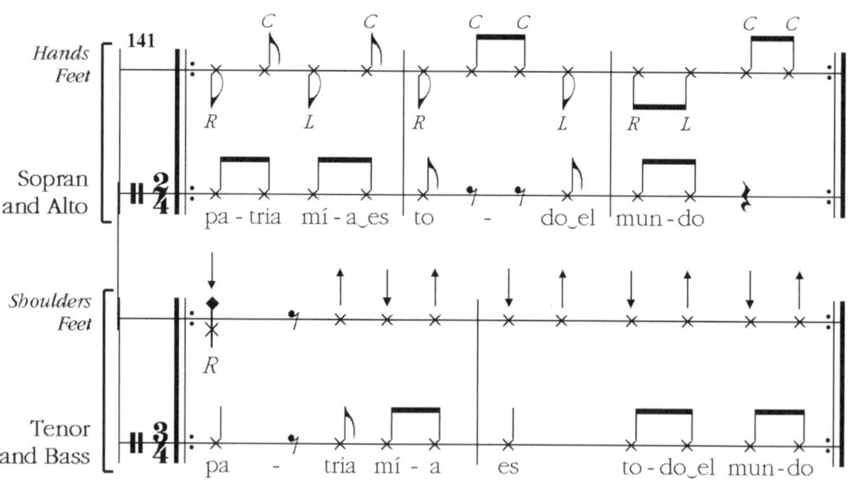

Excerpted from "Mi patria es el mundo" by Alberto Grau (b. 1937 -   ).

Example of Polymeter

The polymeter in this example happens when section A and section B are combined.
Excerpted from "Binnama" by Alberto Grau (b. 1937).

Section A: swing the upper torso and arms forward and backwards (the arrows indicate the direction of the body). Strike the hips with both hands in the first downbeat of this pattern. Fwd. = Forward, Bk. = Backwards.

Section B: bend arms and move them forwards and backwards, opening and closing hands as indicated. Ch = Close hands, Oh = Open hands in front.

Motive

Motive is the organization of successive notes into a unity of a higher order. The synthesis of progressively larger musical structures can only be achieved by juxtaposing smaller elements that are themselves complete. These elements of short duration that are nonetheless coherently whole are motives. They are the basic threads from which the musical fabric is woven. *Cántico,* by Maestro Vicente Emilio Sojo is an example of how motives are combined to form musical phrases.

Example of motive
Section taken from "Cántico" by Vicente Emilio Sojo (1887-1974)

Melody

Understood as an ordered succession of musical sounds, organized by rhythm and register, a melody, no matter how simple, must abide by a series of interpretative rules determined by musical topography and phrasing. Every melody is defined by its rhythmic and harmonic profile. When interpreting a melody it is important to keep in mind the concept of high and low points, and, in the presence of text, to consider the words as an important starting point. From there every conductor should follow the conventions of interpretation according to the rules of musical and poetic phrasing.

Melody has a similar organization to that of the grammatical phrase, and cannot be composed by a single sound without elaboration. It has a starting point, and travels towards a point of greater tension, coming eventually to a resting point, much like the movement of waves or wind. A melody or melodic fragment can be made up of individual notes for each syllable (syllabic style) or written in a more florid style with multiple notes for each syllable (melismatic style).

Melismatic Style

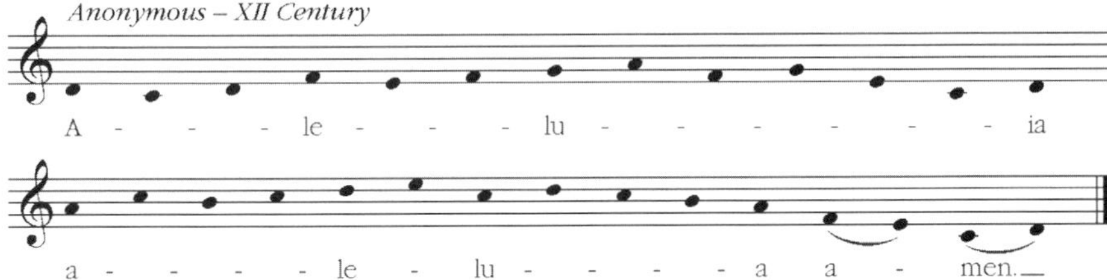

Syllabic Style

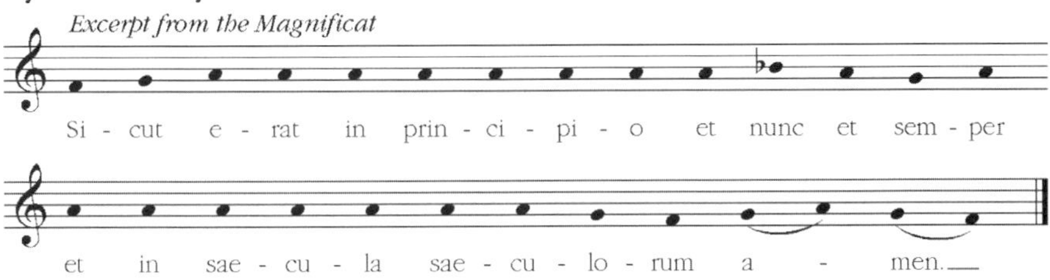

Example of a florid and arpeggiated melody

Melody taken from the second movement from the "Symphony of Psalms"
by Igor Stravinsky (1882-1971)

It is important to remember that melody moves in only one direction—forward. It should comply with traditional norms of interpretation, which can be modified in particular cases to obtain specific or unexpected results or effects. A melody must therefore be coherent, and its interpretation must pursue only one goal: musical expression.

In music, melodic flow can proceed unobstructed, or in some cases it can be interrupted. A melody is like a river that flows calmly where banks are wide, but can easily become violent and agitated where rapids occur.

Harmony and rhythm are sources of support for the outpouring of the melodic discourse, creating or releasing tension as the composer chooses.

Music and Text

If music is combined with lyrics, as is most often the case in choral music, the conductor must take great care to observe the relationship between music and poetry. The issue of the hierarchy of music and text, which impassioned proponents of the rival composers Gluck and Puccini in the 18th century, remains a current debate today. Frequently, climactic points in choral music are based on the poetic text, and in the various genres of vocal music, from opera to *Lied*, rhetoric would claim that there is great correspondence between text and accompaniment. The same can be said for everything from the first Gregorian chants to the music of the *trouvères* and *Minnesänger*, to the Renaissance madrigal, and to opera and oratorio. Even in Wagnerian drama, the guiding principle appears to be an instrumental commentary that supports, contextualizes and elucidates the libretto.

However, conductors must look deeper than the superficial text-melody-accompaniment connection. They must read and understand all the implications of the poetry, regardless of the language. They must know if what is being said is truly what the text means to express, or if there is a hidden double meaning. Once acquainted with the words, they must identify the melody or group of melodies in which that text is transmitted. They must study how the meaning can be best communicated by means of the written score. They must find the proper cadence of the phrases, the words that need to be emphasized, whether through their elongation or by diminishing the weight of the other words that surround them, in order to project the message in the most appropriate way.

Nicolette by Maurice Ravel (1875-1937) is an example of a melody that changes its character in relation to the text.

Example

Excerpted from "Nicolette" from "Trois Chansons" by Maurice Ravel (1875-1937)

First verse – with a joyful and carefree character

Second verse – with a character that describes a growling old wolf

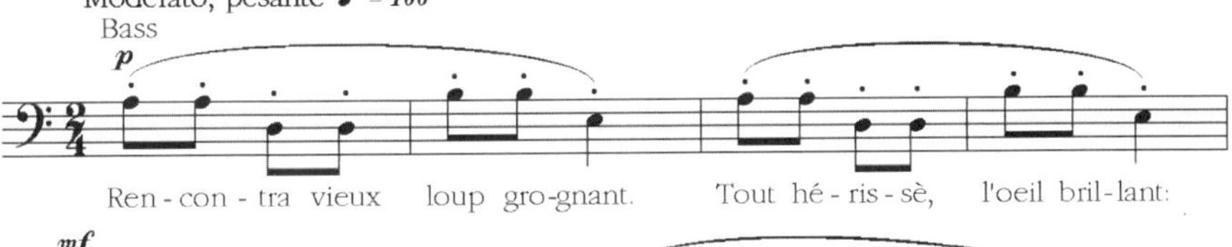

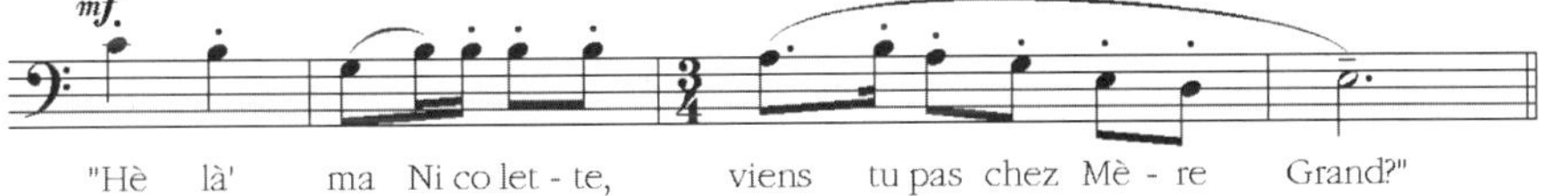

Third verse – description of a sweet, loving and tender page

The timbre of the voices must change according to each of the situations represented in the text. Each person that Nicolette meets on her journey to Grandmother's house has his own character.

Tension and Intensity

Music is nothing but a continuous interplay between intensity and release. The infinite interrelations can be reduced to four essential ones:

1. Low tension with low intensity (ti)

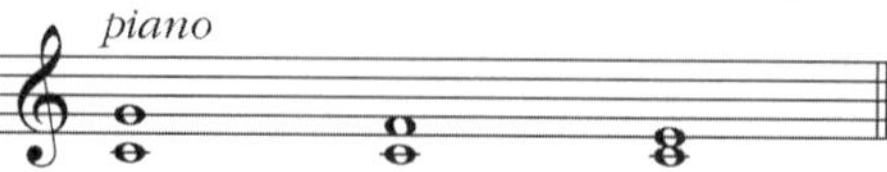

2. Low tension with high intensity (tI)

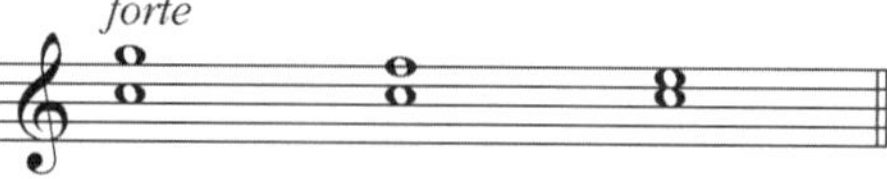

3. High tension with low intensity (Ti)

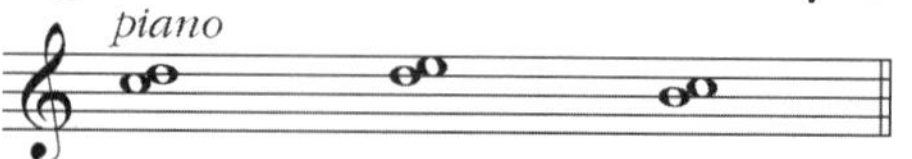

4. High tension with high intensity (TI)

Intensity is music's own intrinsic strength, and phrasing is a constant dialogue between tension and release. The natural tendency is a direct relationship between intensity and register in which higher notes imply greater intensity, and lower notes imply relaxation or release. This is not a hard and fast rule, however, as other musical elements can modify this tendency in surprising and effective ways.

A conductor must take into careful account the rests written in the score. Just like the notes that precede and follow they are part of the phrasing, maintaining, increasing or resolving the energy of the surrounding phrases. In most cases the role of the rest is evident as good composers will incorporate it into the surrounding musical fabric.

Similarly, the complete duration of sustained chords, especially final chords, must be observed in its entirety without rushing, as the duration will be equally related to the natural phrasing of the music. The conductor's intuition serves as the best guide in these cases.

The interplay of musical elements and the intensity they create are manifest in the interaction of the energy of the performer with the score. The conductor must know how to reinforce this energy and transmit it with the greatest efficiency. Knowing how to manage intensity is the key to ensuring a successful performance.

Tessitura and Balance

Just as in orchestral scores we sometimes find combinations that are impossible to balance, a *fortissimo* by a trombone versus a flute, oboe or viola, for example, we also see problems of this sort in choral scores, especially when the composition does not follow rules of tessitura. For example, fast-moving passages in the lower register combined with long notes in the rest of the ensemble and a general dynamic of *forte* will not be successful. Similarly, if the sopranos sing in a low register and the basses and tenors sing *forte* in their higher registers it will be difficult to achieve a good balance. Such extreme examples often occur even in the works of great masters, as seen in the following examples.

Mistaken voicing

Excerpt from the fourth movement of the Ninth Symphony by Ludwig van Beethoven (1770-1827)

It is evident that Beethoven thought of a continuous *crescendo* from the beginning of this passage. But this build-up is interrupted by the entrance of the altos in very low register. This mistake can be fixed by supporting the entering voice part with neighboring voices, such that basses sing with the tenors, the tenors with the altos, etc.

In compositions for equal voices or children's choirs there are often mistakes of this sort. The conductor must find solutions to support the weakest section, sometimes working against what the composer has written. Such difficulties can be the result of carelessness, or possibly because the composer wrote the work in historical circumstances different from the ones we currently live in. For example, in most contemporary choirs the number of the sopranos and altos has increased in relation to the number of tenors and basses.

The question of how to interpret, or possibly re-interpret the original score requires deep reflection. Careful decisions about how to organize the voices to achieve the desired result are essential if one is to discover the best qualities in each composition.

Timbre

Every instrument produces a characteristic sound resulting from the combination of harmonics that constitute its timbre or tone color. By knowing the technical and expressive possibilities of each instrument the conductor will facilitate their best performance. Although the timbres of human voices are less differentiated than those of the orchestra, the possibilities for creativity are infinite. Singers can project wildly varying colors in every register from a deep growling bass to the whistle tones sung by sopranos or children.

In one sense the variation in timbre of voices in a choir is comparable to that of the string family. However the choral ensemble is better paired because unlike in the string quartet in which the sound of each instrument duplicates or emulates that of the violin, in the mixed choir the qualities of the four sections are well matched, but still individually defined.

The conductor must also be conscious of timbre in relation to the historical, stylistic, and even geographical origins of the piece to be interpreted. It would be incorrect to sing always in the same way or with the same timbre, even if it were considered extremely beautiful.

Schola Cantorum de Venezuela, Alice Tully Hall, Mostly Mozart Festival,
New York, EE.UU., 2009. Conductor: María Guinand

Cantoría Alberto Grau, 50th Anniversary ACDA, National Convention,
Oklahoma City, EE.UU., 2009. Conductor: Luimar Arismendi

Chapter 6

Technical Aspects
of Conducting

Gesture and its Importance

"It is true that gesture is one of the most
unique aspects of an actor's personal
language. The first thing I teach to my students
is that gesture, whether bold or subtle,
always precedes the spoken word,
and reveals the actor's emotional state
and intention to communicate."

Vittorio Gassman

Gesture is the basic and most important means of communication between a chorus and its conductor. It transmits the basic pulse of the music and organizes the musical material in a coherent way. Employing a broad variety of movements the director can communicate an authentic and profound interpretation of a musical work.

Through gesture the conductor has the ability to connect with the choir on both a technical and expressive level. Conducting gestures are made up of a fixed, yet variable code that helps the choir decipher the meaning of the music and its internal rhythm and expression. Gesture must therefore be sufficiently clear to avoid any confusion, and adaptable to issues that could arise due to the venue, size of the ensemble, or any other matter. Developing these gestures requires physical practice on the part of the conductor, and learning to recognize and respond to them calls for constant practice between conductor and ensemble.

Gesture will be most useful and expressive when it is fluid and natural. Sometimes, however, one must sacrifice expressiveness for precision, especially when working with orchestral groups that do not play from memory and thus require clear gestures in order to count measures and extended rests.

The theory of gesture must take into account the following aspects:

- The first beat is always represented by a downward motion, as it is associated with the force of gravity.
- Conductors must become conscious of the weight and force of their arm so as to maintain control of tension, intensity and musical nuance.
- Each inflection point or ictus must be marked with a downward motion in which the gestural energy is released. The conductor then prepares the next beat by controlling the speed between each pulse.
- All beats should be placed on the same horizontal plane, which must remain constant in order to maintain clarity of intention. Likewise the height of the gesture in relation to the ground and the distance from body must remain consistent. Consistency in breadth of gesture is also desirable.
- There is a direct relationship between the amplitude of the gesture, the energy used in the movement of the arms, and the interpretation of the piece.
- The sense of flow in the gesture must be continuous, and should be interrupted only in extraordinary cases.
- The tempo must remain constant, even though the speed of the arm travelling different distances between beats may vary. Conductors who are inattentive to this generate confusion and insecurity in the signers.
- It is the music itself that defines a change in direction, amplitude or plane of the gesture.
- The tendency to subdivide or articulate the gesture more becomes increasingly evident after a high point in the phrase. When we approach the nadir of the phrase, tension and intensity generally diminish, and more convergence and parallelism exist.

- Every pattern can be subdivided on each of its sides, and all subdivisions should be done in the same direction as the main beat.

Body Language

The conductor must establish a conduit of communication with the audience and the ensemble. This connection, which should be not only physical but also spiritual-emotional, is based on the following two overlapping criteria:

- First, a clear and fluent gestural technique, which requires a great deal of practice to perfect (patterns, articulations, dynamics, etc.).
- Second, more difficult and subtle, an internal energy through which the conductor seeks to establish an intense and deep contact with the group, allowing every message contained in the music to spring authentically to life.

In practice these two aspects must be woven together to become one. Internal energy and clear technique must work synergistically for the best interpretative result. Any conductor who hopes to be successful must practice and combine musical knowledge with talent, discipline, determination and passion. All of these virtues are essential because conducting, either choral or orchestral, is a career that demands total commitment. Whoever fails to understand this can never be more than a mediocre dilettante in artist's clothing.

Conductors who do not appreciate the necessity of applying themselves fully to elements of bodily or gestural expression will always be less capable than other professionals that have intensely practiced gesture in all its aspects. As there is often more than one way to beat a measure or show a musical passage the conductor must always be prepared to subject the music and the gesture to rigorous study, and, if a better way of showing a passage is discovered, it should be used with the ensemble.

For a choral or orchestral conductor well defined gesture is essential, but it is equally important that other aspects of physical communication not be forgotten. Body language communicates attitude and informs the atmosphere of the rehearsal or performance. Internal positive energy, communicated through active and engaging body language, energizes the singers and gives them the strength that they need to achieve their best. At the most basic level a good conductor must be an indivisible unit of technique and internal spirituality, capable of communicating the most varied interpretations and feelings to the ensemble.

Gestural Technique

All of the ideas mentioned above presuppose knowledge of a basic gestural technique and code used to represent musical language.

The Four Basic Patterns

Gestural technique is not limited to knowing and using conducting patterns. It is not enough to be able to conduct varying metrical combinations, to use a gesture to depict *legato, staccato, crescendo* or *diminuendo*, or to master cues and fermatas. In addition to these technical elements, conductors must develop an actor's ability to project emotion, that indispensable component that enables them to move the singers and audience.

There are four metrical patterns. When conducting them it is important to maintain the same arm height, unless interpretative details indicate otherwise. Because the gesture is derived from the articulatory and rhythmic elements of the music, the number of combinations is infinite.

Sometimes confusion arises when a measure in four is written in two or the other way round. When measures are incorrectly written, the conductor must use gesture to accentuate the places that logically correspond to the phrasing.

Some diagrams of each meter are presented below. They are drawn for right-handed conductors. If conducting with the left hand, the pattern is a mirror image.

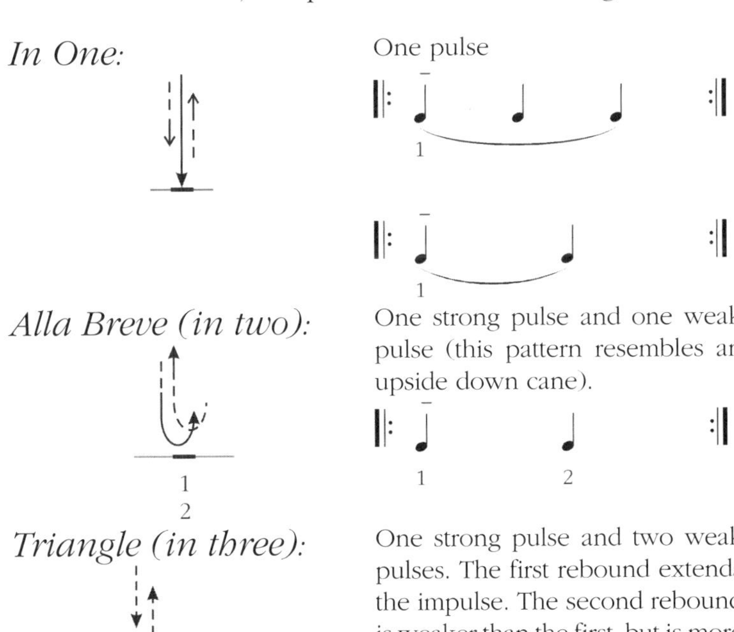

In One:

One pulse

Alla Breve (in two):

One strong pulse and one weak pulse (this pattern resembles an upside down cane).

Triangle (in three):

One strong pulse and two weak pulses. The first rebound extends the impulse. The second rebound is weaker than the first, but is more extended or broad as it prepares the forthcoming downbeat.

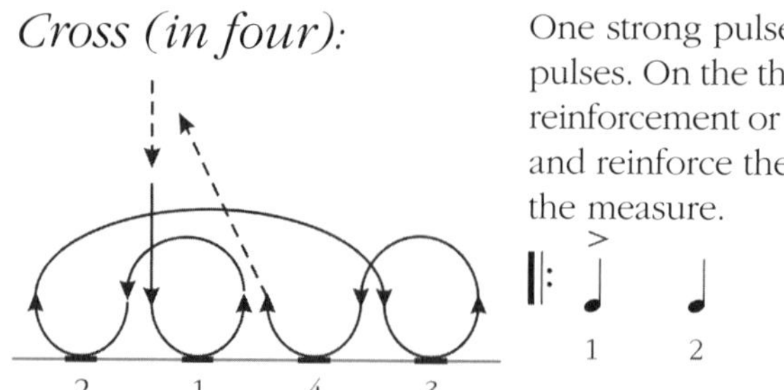

One strong pulse and three weak pulses. On the third beat there is a reinforcement or accent to balance and reinforce the binary nature of the measure.

These four patterns also form the basis for asymmetrical meters. More examples are shown in Appendix.

Balance and proportion between gesture and music

A conductor, through movement, creates a sort of drawing or three-dimensional design. These movements, unique to each director, can be photographed or represented in a diagram. The entire arm from the shoulder to the fingers creates an individual choreography that should be clear enough to be understood and responded to successfully.

In orchestral conducting the conductor's baton facilitates and accentuates the design of the movements in space, clarifying the pattern and assisting the performers to better comprehend the gesture. It is easier to draw and design with the baton, but one can be more expressive when gesturing with only arms and hands. Energy flows more readily through the fingers, lending the conductor the air of a wizard who magically transmits the musical message to the performers. In order to complete this transmission, there must not be any unevenness in the gesture. Conductors cannot allow themselves to lose unity of movement; otherwise they will confuse the performers through gestural incoherence.

Two schools of thought, the German (Prussian) and the French, have defined what is considered to be proper gesture. The German school demands movement that, first and foremost, should be precise and clear. The German tradition promotes an angular gesture, marking beats like cardinal points in space joined by straight lines. Between each of these points, the preferred path is as short as possible. This, no doubt, is a clear way of conducting, but can be rigid and inexpressive.

By contrast, the French school, inherited from the practice of Gregorian chant, also known as the "chironomic" or "hand-expressive school", focuses on circular movements. This is a highly expressive technique that may result in a fuzzy conducting, especially when it comes to defining rhythmic pulse and subdivisions, which must be clearly articulated in space in order to be comprehensible.

Today, the preferred conducting technique involves a combination of the best aspects of these two influences, maximizing their positive aspects while minimizing their defects. This hybrid technique enables the conductor to "play" the choir or orchestra as they would an instrument. If the conductor has learned this technique properly, an efficient connection between the conductor and the members of the choir is possible. If a conductor has not yet learned the appropriate balance between expression and clarity, this task must be undertaken as soon as possible so that gesture becomes second nature and personal. When this is mastered gesture becomes a vehicle for ideas, depth of thought, and sensitivity, enabling the choir to follow phrasing, dynamics, agogic shaping, articulation and all other details of expression.

Beat

The action of marking the rhythm in previously established points of the pattern is called "beat," or "beating time".

Aside from the normal beat, there are three additional types:

Anticipated Beat

This is the name given to the gesture that for musical reasons breaks the symmetry of the pattern by anticipating the following inflexion point. This allows the conductor to reinforce asymmetrical rhythms.

Derived Beat

This is the name given to the gesture that is produced in the same direction of the principal beat within the pattern. It is used to subdivide the pulse that is being marked, allowing the conductor to cue or bring out musical detail in a complicated texture.

Delayed Beat

This is the name given to the gesture that lengthens one of the inflexions of the pattern, delaying the movement towards the following pulse. This is done to clarify melodic movement, to avoid beating insensitively through a passage, or to initiate a *rallentando.*

These exercises must be frequently practiced, modifying inflexion points and the direction of the arm such that the conductor can apply them in any situation.

Preparations, cut-offs and fermatas

Because the technique of showing preparations, cut-offs and fermatas is closely linked, it is best to study and get to know them together.

Preparations

The conductor is strongly advised to combine the action of breathing with the preparation. This helps the singer to perceive the preparatory intention with more clarity and precision.

Just as at the beginning one must use a preparation, at the end one must use a cut-off. This is why it can be said that the end is a consequence of the beginning; or, in other words, there is no end without a beginning as these two moments belong to a single musical unity.

There are two types of preparations:
- The dynamic preparation, a pointed gesture produced on the beat preceding the entrance. It shows the dynamic level of the music to come.

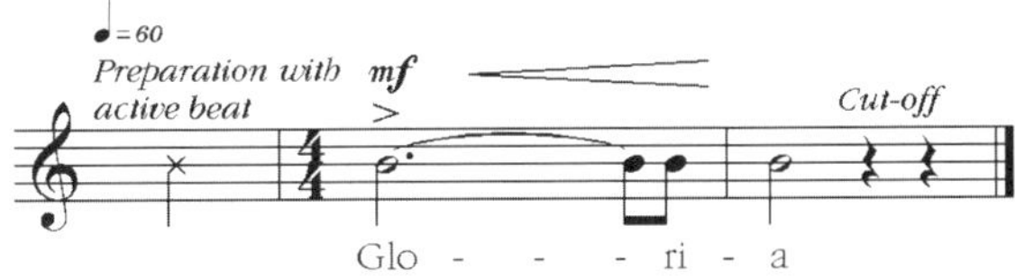

- The expressive preparation, which starts from the pulse immediately preceding the one to be marked, at the level previously established. It is clear without being sharply defined.

The preparation must always be related to:
- The speed or pulse of the music
- The beginning of the piece or a section, the appearance of a new voice, a change of *tempo* or character, or to restart the music after a fermata
- The character, dynamic, intensity, and articulation of the coming passage
- In mixed meter the preparation should be shown in the shortest division of the pulse.

Examples of preparations

Melody taken from "Alleluia" by Randall Thompson (1899-1984)
Accompany each preparation with a breath from the conductor

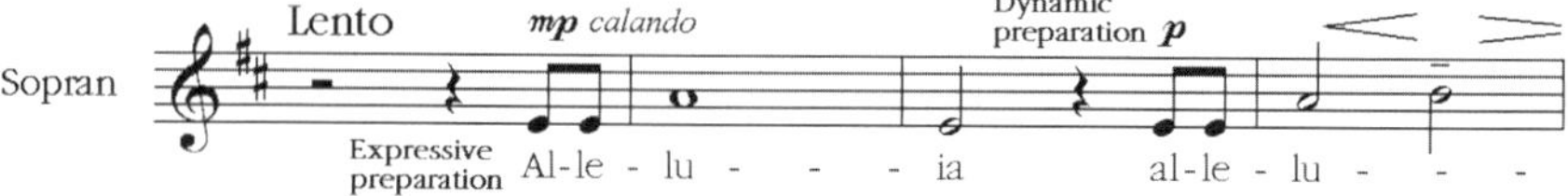

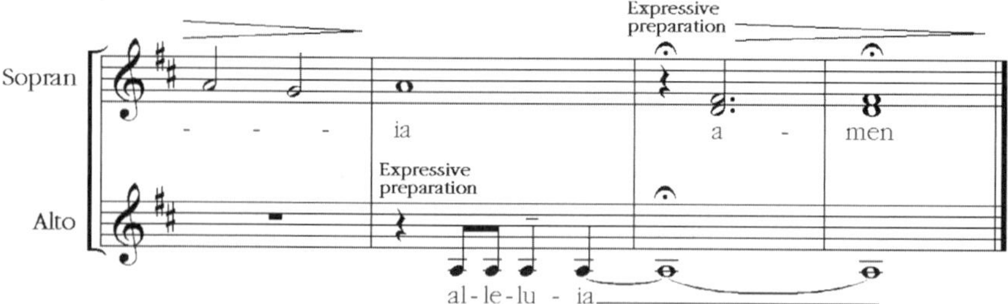

Preparation example and exercise
Melody taken from "La Doncella" by Alberto Grau (1937-)
Accompany each preparation with a breath from the conductor

Cut-offs

Except in those moments in which music progressively diminishes until disappearing (in Italian, *a niente*) a cut-off is appropriate. As with the preparation one must maintain a relation between character, intensity and accumulated tension in this gesture. If the ending is *forte* the cut-off movement will be broad and energetic. If, on the contrary, music ends in a series of delicate chords, the cut-off must adapt to the expressive requirements of the score.

It is impossible to fully catalogue or define the variety of possible preparatory and cutoff gestures. Music, like our own lives, is ever changing. A moment, once lived, can never be truly duplicated. Because of this, it is the conductor's responsibility to be well grounded in gesture and interpretation in order to be able to respond effectively to the musical needs of the moment.

Fermatas

Sometimes the composer will choose to interrupt the musical flow of a piece by holding out a note, chord or rest. In these moments the pause is indicated by a fermata. From a gestural standpoint it is important to remember that every preparatory gesture after a fermata must be contrary to the direction of the beat to be shown. This is also the case with changes of time signature, accents, and rhythmic patterns.

In his chorales, Bach used fermatas to indicate not only extensions of a chord, but also breaths. In these cases the duration of the fermata is determined by the poetic flow, the emphasis of an important word, and the conductor's intuition and musical taste:

Fermata examples and exercises
with cut-offs and preparations

Just as one must always be attentive to expression and quality of the gesture, it is also important to maintain musicality when dealing with fermatas. It is equally inexpressive to shorten a fermata as it is to make it too long.

When conducting fermatas, one must take into consideration the following:

- After a fermata, the preparation must be shown in the same direction as the beat on which the fermata rested.
- At the fermata, if one of the voices continues for more than one pulse, the conductor must continue to beat time.
- The length of a fermata greatly depends on the tension and intensity of the music that leads up to it.

There are a number of possible ways to treat fermatas. The length of the fermata cannot be measured with mathematical precision, rather it is the interpreter's intuition that must determine it. Some educators suggest that a fermata should always last twice as long as the rhythmic figure on which is rests. This rigidity is unmusical and a more flexible approach to the duration of fermatas is recommended.

We have said that fermatas can be resolved in several different ways, which could be classified into four main groups:

Fermata without a cut-off (expressive)

A fermata may or may not have a cut-off. In cases where the music continues without a break the pulse must be reestablished through a preparatory gesture that does not interrupt the subsequent connection. In these cases a breath or cut-off in the gesture must be avoided. In order to not interrupt the music and maintain the desired sonority an expressive preparation must be used.

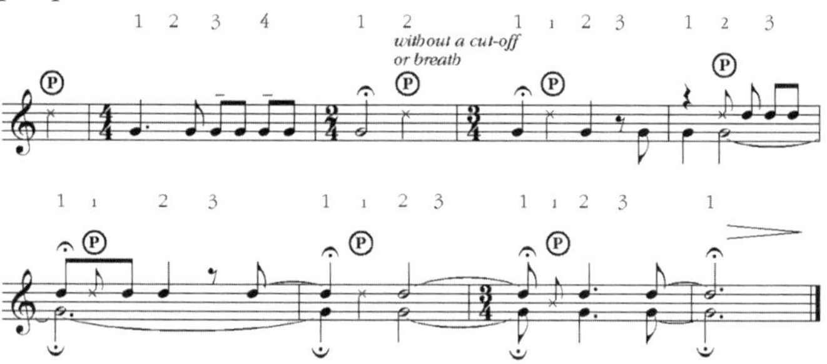

Fermata with cut-off/preparation (dynamic)

In this case the fermata is interrupted with a cut-off, which simultaneously serves as the preparation for the continuation of the new phrase. A dynamic preparation is used here.

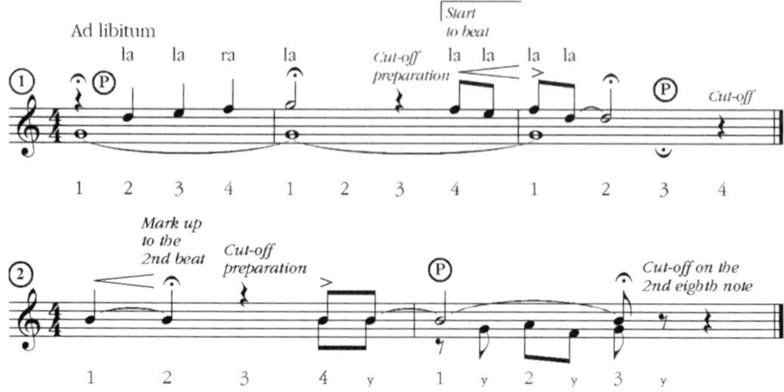

Fermata with cut-off, rest and new preparation

In this case the fermata must be ended with a clear gesture and a new preparation occurs after a pause. A dynamic or expressive preparation can be used as appropriate to the music that follows.

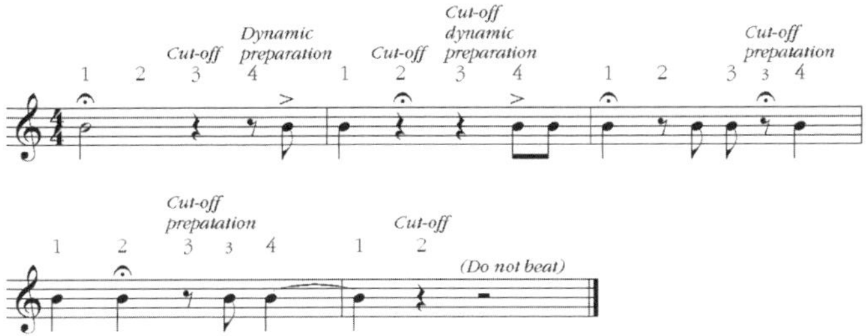

Fermata on the measure bar or on a rest

Here the music is interrupted, producing a rest whose length is determined by musical taste, and the intensity of what has preceded it. A dynamic or expressive preparation can be used accordingly.

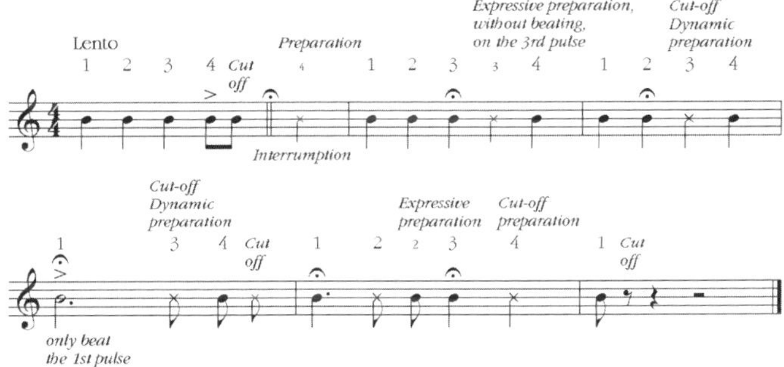

Intensity, color and frequency of fermatas

A conductor must keep in mind that the greater the intensity of the music, the longer the duration of the fermata. There is also a directly proportional relation between greater intensity and greater harmonics, meaning that when the number of simultaneous sounds of different frequencies is greater, more time is needed to grasp the richness of the sounds.

There is no direct relation between pitch and duration of fermatas unless we take into account a simultaneous combination of high and low pitched sounds, as these require more time to be heard and appreciated. If this time is not allowed, the listener cannot assimilate the composer's idea, and expression and interpretive quality suffer. Duration of fermatas and determination of tempo in general must be a manifestation of the conductor's intuition and good criteria, and not the product of empty virtuosity or unthinking reproduction of others' interpretations.

All tempo indications (both in words or metronome marks) must be carefully examined rather than slavishly accepted. There are occasions where a piece can benefit from a departure from the tempo that the composer has indicated. It also must be taken into account that some tempo indications set by a composer centuries ago might not be appropriate or recommendable nowadays. The conductor must understand the relationship between the tempo that is written and the content of the message.

Intonation

"Intonation is like the color of the rose"

Robert Shaw[34]

The tonal system of half and whole steps used by our western culture has, in a way, defined our sense of intonation, in which we distinguish up to the tempered semitone. Smaller intervals, such as third- or quarter-tones, are not perceived with equal ease, and are considered "out of tune" pitches.

---

[34] Robert Shaw (1916-1999). Conductor and patriarch of interpretation in choral music in USA. He transformed the art of choral conducting and rised its standards.

Just as we encounter musicians that are conscious and capable of singing in tune, there are other singers that do not clearly distinguish perfect intonation. Just as a singer trains with vocalization exercises, it is advisable to expose young musicians to the indispensable discipline of accurate intonation as part of their early musical training. While it is true that singers must have deep knowledge of the mechanisms of the vocal apparatus (diaphragm, lungs, vocal cords, etc.), they must be also conscious that all these organs are under the aegis of their intelligence, for in the end the system is governed by thought. Thus the singers' intelligence holds sway over the mysterious practice of intonation, a phenomenon that, among others, distinguishes the human race from any other living species.

Here are some practical exercises mainly recommended for children's and youth choirs to train the difference between exact and approximate intonation.

Once these intonation exercises have been rehearsed with long and *legato* figures, they can be practiced with rhythmic figures, for example:

Starting with a reference pitch sung by half of the choir, the other half is asked to sing different intervals, concentrating carefully before singing that new sound. It is possible that the intonation will not be perfect in all the members of the group, but after identifying the children that still cannot match pitch within the choir, the conductor must ask them to listen to the more capable singers in order to become aware of their difficulty and correct it. These exercises can also be done in the middle of a rehearsal using sections that are difficult to perform, using the better voices as models for the rest of the group.

These exercises can also be done with adult choirs. Logically, had they been exposed to this training as youngsters, adults would likely be more secure in matters of intonation. Sometimes we hear professional singers that regretfully have not been able to solve their intonation problems, and moreover are incapable of correcting it as they focus on purely physical issues, ignoring the important intellectual aspect.

We also frequently hear conductors giving inaccurate pitches at the beginning of an *a cappella* piece. When the group leader cannot guarantee giving the correct pitches to the choir, it is better to find other means to give pitches to the group.

There is a small percentage of people for whom it is almost impossible to sing off pitch. There is another, larger percentage that can achieve accurate intonation through practice and study. A third group will have a hard time with intonation for a variety of reasons, including shyness, ignorance, carelessness, lack of a training method, etc.

All this explanation is intended to highlight the complex situation that choral conductors face. Though they frequently feel unable to correct patterns of bad intonation that are so deeply rooted in our choral societies it is nonetheless worth insisting that any human being can learn to sing in tune, provided enough time and patience, and a strong desire to learn.

Score Study

The study of the score must be done from the general to the specific, from the whole to the parts, arriving finally at the smallest musical building blocks.

The initial study will comprise a review of the primary climatic points. A climatic point is never a vertical instant, but a surface, a wide horizontal dimension. The energetic rise and fall of and musical piece will generally be related to concepts of divergence, contrast and heterogeneity within the score. As the climactic point approaches contrast will diminish and convergence and parallelism will be reinforced. These climactic points are necessarily set off by sections of lesser intensity.

Harmony should be studied by analyzing its development over the course of the piece. Generally the harmonic flow is designed to support melodic requirements in a composition. All melodic functions should be analyzed in terms of increasing or decreasing tension. Recurring patterns should be observed, as should any variation in the repetition that should be brought out. Handling patterns according to their natural tendencies is central to ensuring interpretive quality. The main theme must be located, and also the place where it appears with maximum intensity. Any contrasting themes must be discovered.

Writing a musical arrangement

Without a doubt, the conductor who sets out to write an arrangement must keep in mind that a good rendering does not alter the original essence of the work. The arranger should:

- Pay attention to the range and tessitura in each section, taking into account the capabilities of the members of the ensemble for which the arrangement is intended.
- Distribute the melody within the voices in a way that it can be heard and not lost due to poor voicing or polyphonic complexity.
- Observe beforehand what is unique about the work and the text, and note which elements could be exploited to generate special effects.
- Determine the harmonic progressions that will be used.

- Define the climatic moments in order to concentrate the greatest tension there.
- Make the rhythm as clear as possible and find the best way to notate it.
- Correctly use the rhythmic profile of the melody, articulating and enriching it in some of the other voices as well.
- Correctly orchestrate or harmonize the original by bringing out the inherent qualities of the melody and text.

Main Hall, Centro de Acción Social por la Música, Caracas, Venezuela, 2009. Verdi's Requiem. Conductor: Helmuth Rilling

Aula Magna, U.C.V. Giuseppe Verdi's Te Deum. Caracas, Venezuela, 2005.
Conductor: Claudio Abbado

Rios Reyna Hall, Teresa Carreño Theater. Gustav Mahler's Second Symphony.
Caracas, Venezuela, 2004. Conductor: Simon Rattle

Rios Reyna Hall, Teresa Carreño Theater. Ludwig van Beethoven's Ninth Symphony.
Caracas, Venezuela, 2004. Conductor: Gustavo Dudamel

Rehearsal Techniques

Rehearsal Techniques

César Ferreyra

Conductors can lead rehearsals and performances without careful planning. In fact this happens frequently, but the final result is invariably of reduced quality. Poor concerts are often explained away as a result of an inexperienced choir or a lack of rehearsal time. Although these excuses are sometimes valid, the responsibility to educate and inspire nonetheless falls to the conductor, who must awaken in the singers a commitment to quality in performance.

It is important to insist on the character of the piece in every rehearsal, focusing especially on the meaning and communication of the text. To this end, diction and articulation of each syllable must be carefully undertaken, and careful attention paid to the shaping of each phrase. The more a singer or interpreter is instructed and understands the interpretative intention of the conductor and the composer, the better the final result will be.

In cases of poor attendance or lateness an immediate solution must be found. The conductor must insist that the choir members arrive on time. New singers must be recruited to replace those that are unable to commit to the ensemble.

A conductor who wishes to achieve the best results should begin with a thorough study of the composition. The next step is to write out a rehearsal plan, which should include a series of vocalizations and rhythmic, interpretive and linguistic exercises designed to facilitate the learning process and address the most important difficulties in the score. It is recommended that the conductor plan carefully before each rehearsal, writing out in detail the pedagogy to be followed.

Score study and rehearsal planning must always take into account the choral or instrumental ensemble at hand. The lower the musical level of the group, the greater the number of tools required to solve problems. Below is an example of an exercise designed to help non German-speaking singers practice the linguistic challenges, and ultimately memorize the fugue of the third movement of the German Requiem by Johannes Brahms.

Memorization example

Fugue of the third movement of the "German Requiem" by Johannes Brahms (1833-1897)

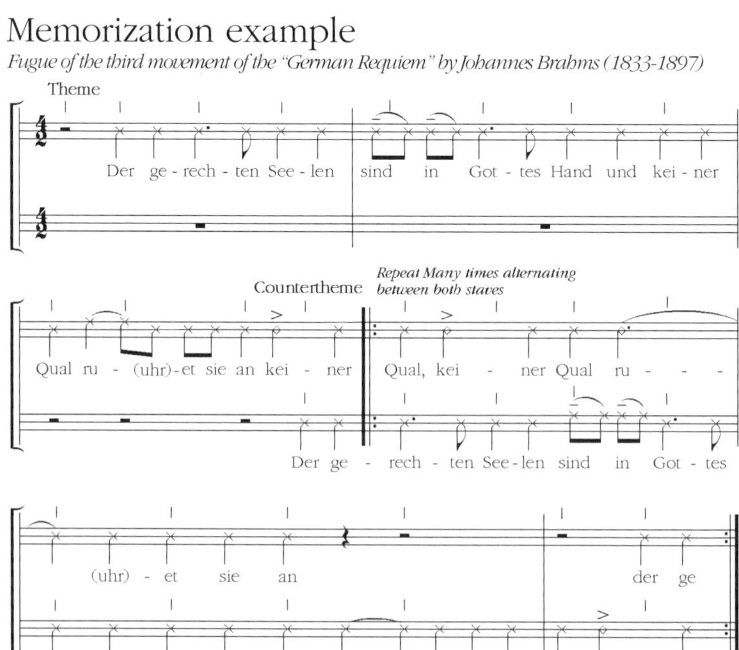

Preparing amateur choirs

Breathing

The conductor must explain the concept of breath flow, and teach the singers how to control it. Metaphors likening breath to a flowing stream, or a column of water suspending a ping-pong ball can be helpful.

Exercises such as lightly blowing a lit candle without extinguishing its flame, panting, or filling and emptying the lungs completely can be used to strengthen the diaphragm. Conductors can learn other techniques through observation of colleagues.

One can also create special exercises, almost like games, to train breathing. For example:

"The Little Train" exercise
Based on compositions by Heitor Villa-Lobos (1887-1959)
and Carlos Alberto Pinto Fonseca (1933-2007)

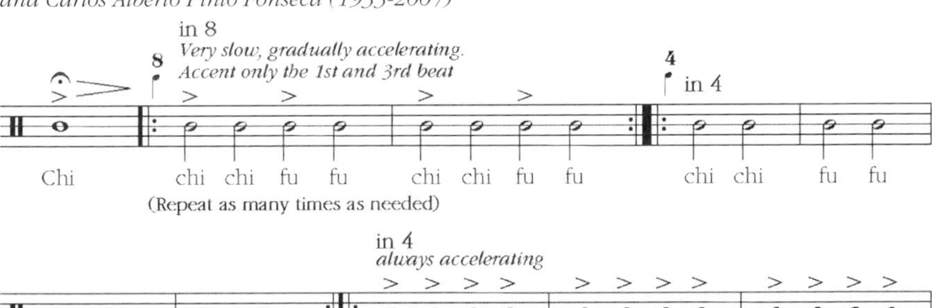

"The Puppy" exercise

With happy face, move hands in front of face and chest
and execute small jumps on the tippy-toes like an excited, begging puppy

"The Swimmer" exercise

Lightly bend the upper torso forward. Breathe and proportionally exhale, moving
the arms in a swimming stroke on each quarter note pulse. Inhale in the last
eighth note of each section, rotating the head to one side, imitating the breathing
of a swimmer. Breathe every 4 – 6 – 8 – 10 strokes

"The Train" exercise

Place both arms at chest level and move them forward with energy.
Feet: mark the rhythm with the heel, without lifting the toes from the floor.

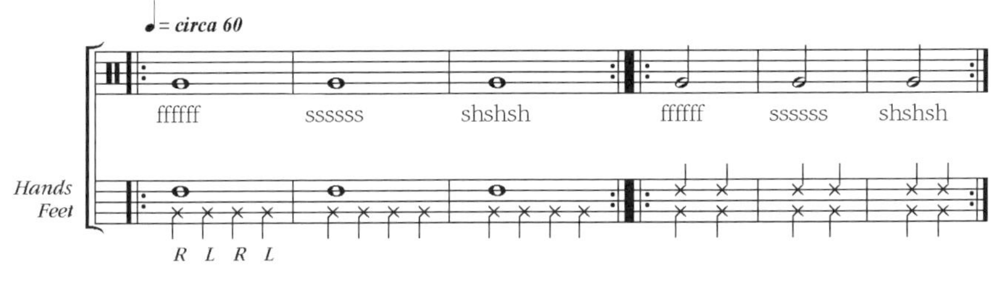

"The Kettle" exercise

Hands on the stomach, applying light pressure on the exhalation but not
on the inhalation. Feet mark the rhythm with the heel, without lifting
the toes from the floor.

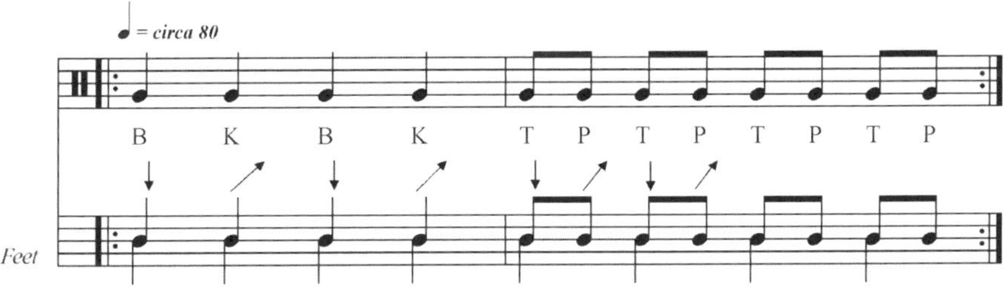

These exercises can be alternated with others, doing one or two each rehearsal.

Vocalization

The best way to prepare a choir vocally and mentally for a rehearsal or performance is through vocalization. This requires knowledge and proficiency that is far from universal.

Conductors who prefer not to vocalize their choir can seek assistance from an expert singer to lead the warm up. Other conductors prefer to lead it themselves. In either case the worst enemy of a good warm up is boredom, most often caused by repetition of the same exercises at each rehearsal. A group of vocalizations and breathing exercises that can be alternated is preferable than a boring session of unchanging scales and arpeggios.

Werner Pfaff, a prestigious German conductor, has a system to start a rehearsal in which he combines melodies in several voices at different speeds. By varying the dynamics with constantly changing gestures Pfaff simultaneously works on vocal preparation and concentration.

The term "warm-up" for vocalization is problematic because the vocal cords are not muscles or tendons. A vocalization exercise activates the voice apparatus, but, more than that, it is an especially useful practice to charge the body with energy and generate healthy tension in the muscles involved in the breathing process. At its best it also serves to generate enthusiasm and energize the ensemble.

It is recommended that the conductor create vocalization exercises based on difficult aspects of a piece (melismas, difficult intervals challenging text, sudden changes of dynamics, etc.). This method requires some planning by the conductor, but is usually appreciated by the choristers who welcome and prefer unique exercises to tedious ascending and descending arpeggios. These rote exercises not only fail to stimulate the choir, but can also generate tension or nervousness, resulting in fatigue and a loss of concentration prior to a rehearsal or performance. Some models of vocalization exercises combined with eurhythmic elements follow:

"The Iguana" exercise

Imitate an iguana crawling forward, with open hands

"Kilón" exercise

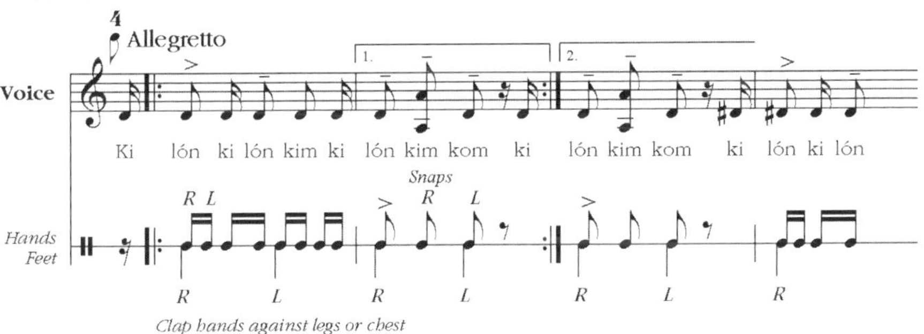

"Ku tum kum" exercise

Hands clapping against chest or legs. R=right hand. L=left hand.
C=clap palms together. Right foot forward – left foot back

"Mi Niño (my child)" exercise

Place arms as if rocking a baby side to side

"Mim mem mam mom mum" exercise

First measure = snapping with both hands.
Second measure = clap both hands against chest or legs

First "Mio" exercise

Bend arms in front of body and do the following: First measure = point to the chest with hands. Second measure = close fists and make swirling motions (S) for crescendo and diminuendo. Conductor can determine the length of the fermata

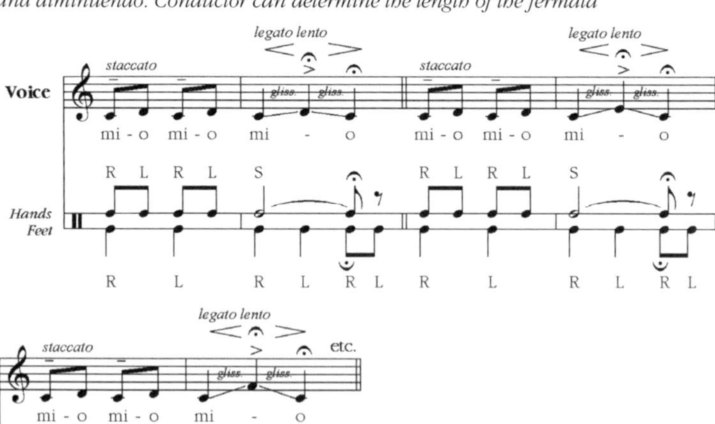

Second "Mio" exercise

First measure = bend arms in front of body and make gentle circular movements.
Second measure = punch left fist against an open right hand

"Tastes and smells" exercise

Gesture with hands as if tasting or smelling something delicious. Resonate the "M"
well.

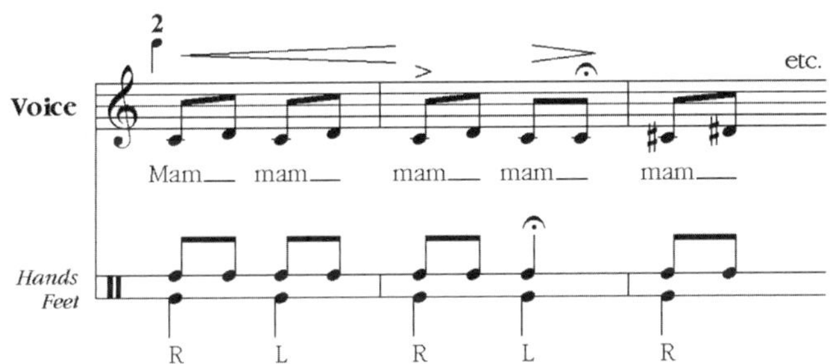

"Tum tum" exercise

Hands against legs as if playing drums. Mark the rhythm in the feet with the heels,
without lifting the toes from the ground.

"Uga uga" exercise

Hands- on the quarter notes reach out as if trying to catch something. On the eighth notes, punch forward

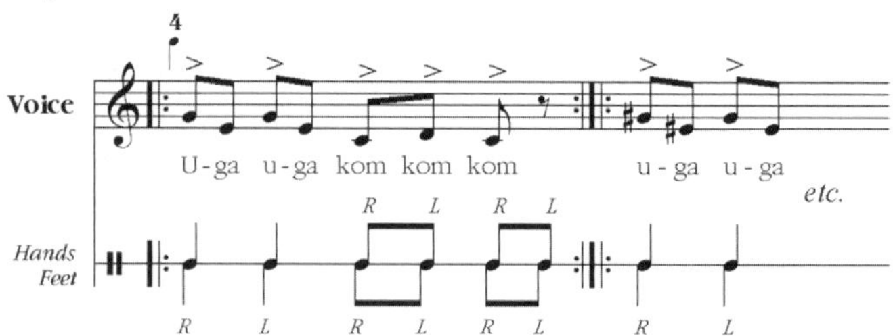

Vocalization can often be less than stimulating. On one occasion, during an activity in a choral conducting class, the students were asked to design a series of vocalization exercises in the manner of "games" which they had to name with funny titles. To evaluate their effectiveness these exercises were to be tested with their respective groups, the majority of which were children's choirs. The students prepared very attractive "exercise-games" full of humor, ingenuity, and innocence and achieved great success with their choirs.

Some time later, all these new conductors but one had returned to the traditional vocalizations, even though the children preferred the new method. The decision to return to the old practice was a question of convenience as the conductors did not want to take the time to create new material. Instead they preferred to follow the daily routine that did not require any intellectual effort.

Following this "path of least resistance" is human nature and to a certain extent understandable, but art and music call us to something greater. In any case, if the creation of this type of material is not possible because of time constraints, or if good pre-existing material that could be useful for this particular purpose can not be found, it is recommended that conductors think of exercises that combine breathing, concentration and dynamics to vocally prepare a choir. It is also important to prepare and energize the body and mind using physical movements, so as to support the vocalization by harmonizing the relationship between voice, breath and body. Although the preceding exercises were originally conceived for children's choirs, they have also been used with adult choirs with excellent results.

Recordings

Nowadays recordings are an essential way for conductors to make their professional work known to others. Recordings are the most convenient way to chronicle the history of a choral ensemble and also its importance within the historical and cultural context of its country. Every conductor should maintain a dossier of recordings to be used both to verify the improvement of their development as a conductor, and testify to the evolution of their artistic maturity.

Live recordings

It is very difficult to achieve a good final product in a live concert unless the sound engineer has professional quality equipment that is adequate for the recording of choral ensembles and is willing to do a sound check in a rehearsal in order to calibrate the microphones. The result of the recording will be unsatisfactory if the hall is not completely soundproof, isolating incoming exterior sounds, or if the audience does not keep an attitude of quiet without interruption from coughing, beeping watches, cell phones, etc.

Because of all of the above, live recordings usually have defects, and are of lesser quality when compared to those done in a recording studio or a hall designed for recordings. In any case, a live recording can be worthwhile if the goal is to have a memory of an unrepeatable moment, for archival purposes, or as a study guide for the conductor who desires to improve.

Studio recordings

The professional history of a conductor can be traced in their performances and recordings, and for recordings to be released to the public the recording studio is recommended so that the conductor and choir are seen in the best possible light. In a studio recording the expectations and tensions of the concert hall are set aside and, without the pressure of a live audience, both conductor and choir are in a more relaxed state of mind. Better concentration, and the luxury of repeating and perfecting each passage as necessary most often yield results superior to live recordings.

Studio recordings are more expensive, and demand excellent preparation from the choir in order to avoid too many repetitions. The argument in favor of the live recording tends to be that it captures more emotion, but one should not forget that wonderful musical moments and excellent focus can also be achieved in the studio, most often with better sound quality.

Completing a number of sessions in a recording studio can be an excellent growth experience for an ensemble. If a choir has the resources to allow this type of work, it is highly recommended, especially for choirs that want to raise their level. Among many advantages, working in this way demands greater concentration from the group and it also allows the conductor to hear the results of each take and correct defects immediately.

Concert hall acoustics

The final result of a concert depends greatly on the quality of the hall or space in which it takes place. The unfortunate reality is that sometimes neither the conductor nor the ensemble has the opportunity to choose the performing venue. It can happen that the people that choose the venues do not have the slightest knowledge of acoustics, and lack any knowledge of the appropriate place for the repertoire to be interpreted. A big church can be excellent for slow-moving music with great dynamic contrasts because the duration of the fermatas in *forte* or *fortissimo* can be extended, creating instants of great intensity and emotion. But that same space will not yield good results if the repertoire includes pieces accompanied by percussion instruments with fast rhythms.

Based on all of the above we can conclude that given the variety of acoustics, from very resonant to very dry, it is appropriate that the conductor should be allowed a say in the selection of the venue. If this is not possible, then the conductor must choose repertoire that suits the acoustics of the venue that has been chosen. Sadly this is often impossible as the repertoire is selected first, and then circumstances require choirs to sing in places that are inappropriate for the repertoire to be interpreted.

So, a conductor must keep in mind the following:
- If there is more reverberation ("wet" acoustics), tempos should be slower.
- If there is little reverberation ("dry" acoustics), tempos should be faster, and long pauses should not be extended.
- If the reverberation is very long, it is sometimes good to search for ways to balance the sections of the choir, often relating to standing position of each section, and the choir's position in the space.

- It is helpful to arrange the choir in such a way that the sections can hear each other well, especially in dry acoustics. This will facilitate intonation, rhythmic precision, and communication among choristers.
- There is an optimal tempo for each acoustic, but to be aware of this is not enough to ensure good results. Theory must be adequately nourished by practice. Experience, previous rehearsals, and careful attention to all details will be the keys to success in dealing with a variety of acoustical issues.

One must give proper attention to acoustics and be adequately prepared to know under which conditions to make modifications to benefit a performance. In some cases the success of a musical work can hinge on the conductor's capacity to modify the performance because of acoustical issues. Through experience and sensitivity the conductor must develop criteria as to when this kind of "emergency improvisation" is necessary.

The choral concert

There is no better way to share the work of a conductor and ensemble than a concert performance.

The choral concert, like any other concert, is a show, and must therefore follow certain norms. The success of a concert depends on many factors other than the quality of the conductor and the ensemble that are, without a doubt, indispensable. A good concert requires appropriate repertoire, adequate acoustic conditions, and interpretative sensitivity that engages the audience and singers on an emotional level.

When reflecting on past performances, conductors are most often not completely satisfied. To the contrary, they typically have no difficulty identifying sections that could have been more successful. The initial enthusiasm one feels on taking on a work is not always matched by an equal sense of satisfaction at the end of the process.

New discoveries in musical performance are rare, but in the visual arts it does happen that a detail can suddenly be discovered, bringing new life to a well-known work and reconnecting the person observing the art to the original idea of the artist. In music there is an additional layer of communication as the performer is the re-creator and conduit for the composer's ideas, which are transmitted to the listener through the rendering of a written score in sound.

Conductors must keep in mind that nowadays their work faces stiff competition from radio, television, computer games, and movies. Television offers concerts by famous orchestras and great soloists. Music lovers, though they miss the emotion of a live concert, need never leave home. Communication via internet and cellular phone, video games, professional sports, and the almost pathological passion of the fans—all of this clashes with the conductor's efforts to attract an audience. This is why, now more than ever, a conductor must be extremely careful in the selection of varied and entertaining repertoire without making any concessions to mediocrity.

As with all art, the appetite of the public changes over time. A score that fascinated them in the past might not be equally successful today, and another that seemed strange or uninteresting might now communicate a message of beauty. Exciting and novel interpretations can bring new life to a piece that was long forgotten.

Indubitably, a concert is a singular experience for choir, conductor and audience. It is an emotional phenomenon, and as such can never be repeated. This is why being a musician requires a constant devotion, as that unique moment, truly profound and heartfelt, will never repeat itself with the same intensity as the first time. Music is a fluid art form that moves through and with time. Once a performance is gone, rather than attempt to recreate it one must instead try to achieve an expressive rendition that is different and new.

Once finished, a concert disappears. The aesthetic effect and the emotion that it generates exist only in memories. Even if a recording is made, it is but a partial reflection of what happened, a snapshot of a unique moment that cannot be recreated authentically and completely because it can not capture the emotion that director, choristers and audience experienced.

Keeping this in mind, a good conductor will never, under any circumstances, try to "repeat" previous success by rendering the piece in the same way as on previous occasions. This will end up being no more than a mechanical and boring performance lacking profundity and spirituality. The mission of a conductor is not fulfilled by flawlessly rendering what is written in a score. A written score does not change, but the person who is sensitive to music, as a conductor should be, will always find a way not to simply repeat past performances. Every new performance offers a chance at re-creation, of finding new and more profound emotions on each hearing. Simple fidelity to the written score can never be enough.

Even if we assume that both conductor and ensemble will always give their best, it is inevitable that some concerts achieve greater success than others. This can be due to any number of factors, including acoustic conditions, sufficient preparation time, better singers, appropriate and attractive repertoire, etc. These aspects must be taken into consideration beforehand to make decisions to ensure the success of the concert.

Aside from the risk of nervous tension already mentioned, another risk that should be taken into consideration is exaggerating the expectations of a performance. If the choir is told that the only expectation is perfection, the group's response might be one of distress, conditioning them beforehand to feel incapable of achieving the success their leader expects. A conductor will equally moderate his discontent regarding unsatisfactory results, because if not, they could lose the motivation of their team, which will cause problems in future performances.

Every artistic ensemble should set the goal of achieving excellent results. In unfavorable conditions, lack of rehearsal time or inexperienced singers, it is best not to set unreachable goals that create false expectations, resulting in unnecessary disillusionment. These considerations are equally valid when preparing a choir to participate in competitions.

Sensitive conductors who with good leadership skills will find that performing simple repertoire in places that lack artistic outlets, such as hospitals, schools, jails, etc., is an important way to raise the spirits of the choir while meaningfully contributing to society and benefiting a community.

Marketing the choral concert

Choral music must attract audiences, rather than putting them off with programs that engender distrust, or rejection. The idea that only high profile concerts can attract an attentive and enthusiastic audience is misguided.

Sometimes conductors are surprised to see the audience's excitement for a song of minimal technical difficulties, in which the imitation of a bird's singing, the rhythm of a train or a funny solo part are enough to charm the audience. This is food for thought, suggesting that it is not always the solemnity or difficulty of the concert that satisfies an audience.

We must recognize that today's audience is frequently comprised of friends and family of choristers. All of us who advocate the continuation and success of choral music would like to have a truly enthusiastic audience that is ready to fill big venues. We would like our halls to be filled to capacity and be enthusiastically cheered on and off stage to great applause, but this is not always the reality.

How can we generate a better and more enthusiastic attendance at our concerts? That is a great challenge that has to be met with courage and sincerity in the near future. If we fail to address this it will be progressively more difficult to catch the attention of the media and the funding of governments and private companies.

If we want it to survive, the choral concert must be modified from the model of the last three centuries. It must undergo an adaptation to the present times. It is vital that we find a better way to generate an artistic movement led by conductors, professional and amateur musicians, members of orchestras and choirs, chamber musicians and soloists of every specialty. Our job is to promote peace and progress, and bring people together through music. There is no call for intolerance, orthodoxies, racism or xenophobia in a choir. Just as with any group of musicians, a choral ensemble can include people from different ideologies and religions as brothers and sisters in artistic endeavor.

Musicians, and choirs in particular, are an example of harmony. However, convivial music-making does not always receive the support of governments and organizations. On the occasion of one of the frequent crises in the Middle East, a project of joint concerts between a Palestinian choir and an Israeli choir was proposed with the intention of demonstrating the brotherhood that should exist between those communities. The project was rejected by both governments.

In a world where family ties are breaking down, and moral standards are declining, people often turn to leisure activities that are destructive. It is therefore more important than ever to advocate for activities that reinforce teamwork, generate strong ties of friendship, develop good taste and aesthetic sensitivity, and reinforce social and artistic values.

Coda

In the preceding pages I have shared some ideas about the path for conductors to follow. These concepts are the product of extensive practical experience and deep reflection. I trust that they will be useful to my future colleagues in this profession that is filled with promise, ever-open horizons, and connections to the deepest realities of our existence.

Readers might agree to a greater or lesser degree with the ideas presented in previous pages that are, without exception, the product of accumulated experience of many years of intense work, study with respected masters, and much reading on the subject of conducting. Everything that I have written has been true for me, and I believe will be useful for anyone who chooses to pursue this field.

This text is based entirely on my own ideas. I have not formulated the "unique and universal method" of becoming a choral conductor because such a method does not exist. I have discussed subjects derived from my academic studies and from my work as a pupil of very qualified conductors to whom I offer a tribute of affection, gratitude and respect. I have offered ideas that are the product of many hours conducting rehearsals and concerts with very diverse choirs in many venues throughout the world.

If this book has any merit, then I have already received much greater recompense over the course of my professional life. It has been given by my choristers, many of them colleagues nowadays, and almost all of them my friends. I will have also received my reward from the audience, to whom I have always tried to give the best of my experience because I felt I owed it to them. My reward has come from the hands of those who have honored me with prizes, distinctions and tributes, and those who have allowed me to serve nationally and internationally in the service of our profession. Allow me to express my gratitude to all of them.

To those who read this book, young artists for whom I sincerely wish these pages can light a path to follow. I hope that in your future you feel, as I did, the impulse to continue in the passionate search for "truth" in the wonderful world of choral conducting, even though it is and always will be unreachable.

Exercises
Appendix
Thematic Index
Index of Examples
and Exercises

Exercises

Exercise 1
Add a text with the word "Amen" to this composition (possible solution on page 182)

Johann Josef Fux
(1660 - 1741)

Exercise 2
Add a text with the word "Alleluia" to this composition (possible solution on page 182)

Johann Josef Fux
(1660 - 1741)

Exercise 3

Choose a text, i.e. "Et in terra pax" or "Da nobis pacem", and use it in a composition to learn how to correctly set a poem to already written music. Sometimes a composition can present inconsistencies between the music and a poetic idea. If the conductor knows how to correct these defects, the final rendition will be better .

Leonardo Leo
(1694 - 1744)

Exercise 4

Practicing setting text to a second and third voice will be useful when correcting texts that have been set inaccurately.

Ave Fénix, International Day of Choir, 2008.
Conductor: Alberto Grau

Exercise 1
Possible solution

Exercise 2
Possible solution

Appendix
Gestures to beat measures

In five (slow) with cross:

Any of the sides can be subdivided,
as appropriate.

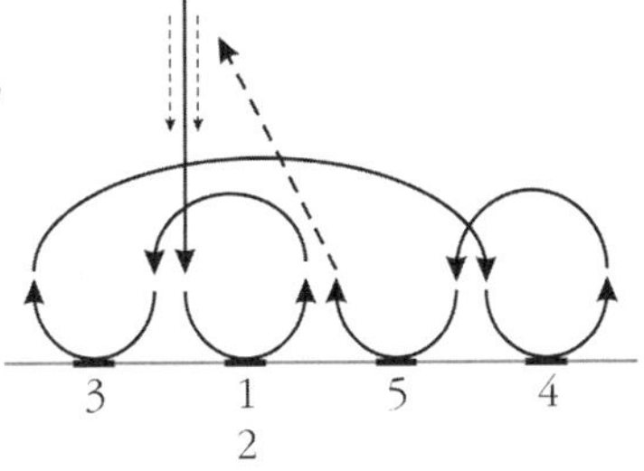

In five (slow) with triangle:

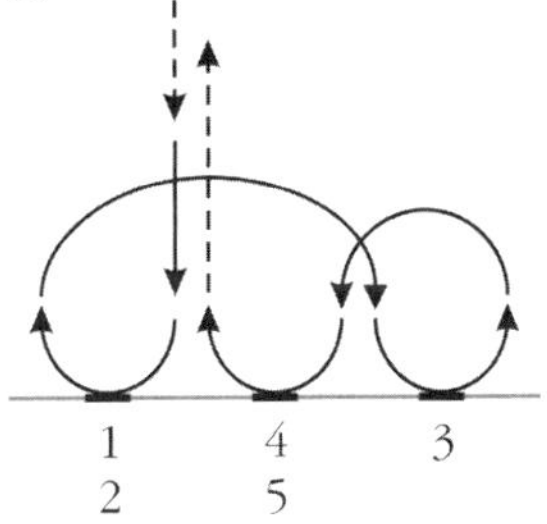

In five (fast) with upside down cane:

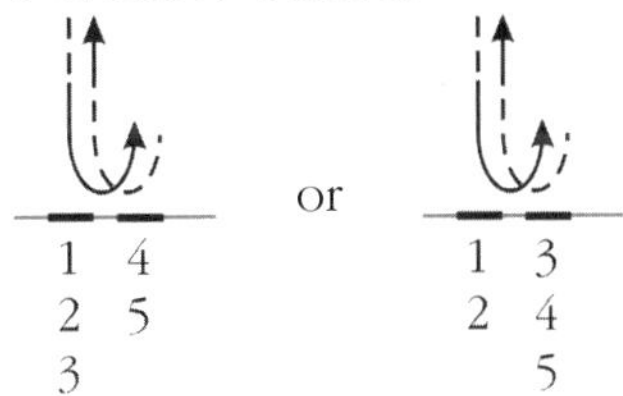

In six (slow) with cross 1:

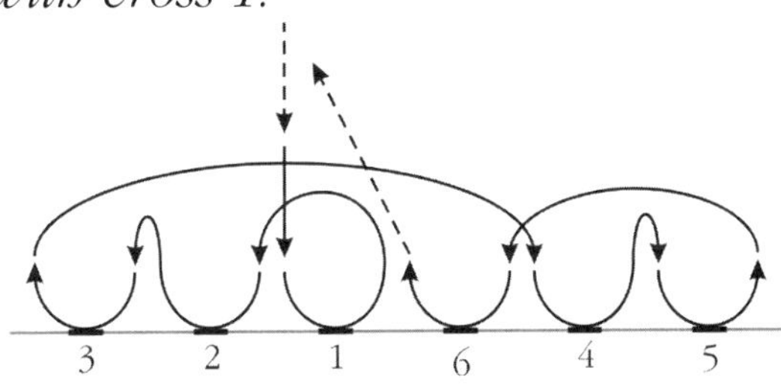

In six (slow) with cross 2:

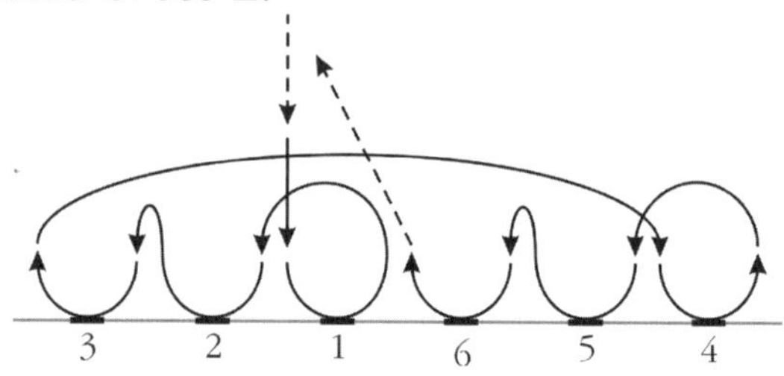

In six (slow) with cross 3:

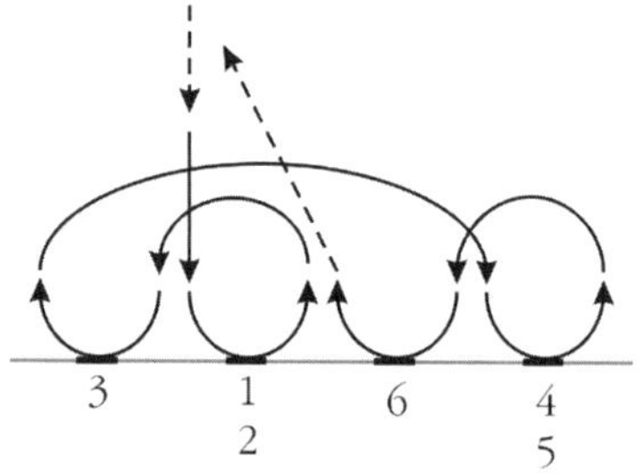

In six (slow) with triangle:

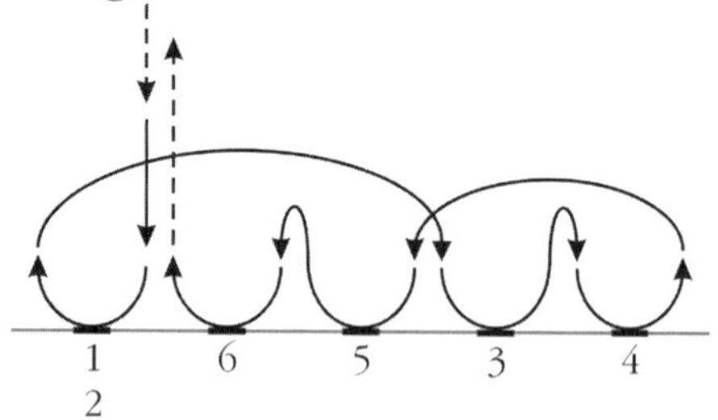

In six (fast) with upside down cane:

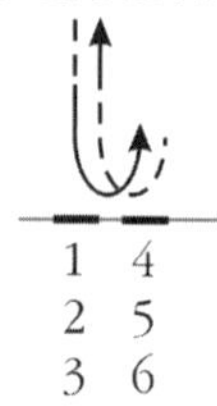